SO... THIS IS HONG KONG

Adventures of an American Who Moved East

Angela D. French

SO… THIS IS HONG KONG

Adventures of an American Who Moved East

The events and conversations in this book were recorded to the best of the author's ability. To protect the privacy of individuals however, some specific characteristics were changed, some events compressed, and some dialogue recreated. No geckos were harmed in the writing of this book.

Copyright © 2021 by Angela D. French

All rights reserved. So seriously, please don't copy, reproduce, distribute, or transmit the material in any form, including photocopying, handwriting, audio recording, smoke signals, telegrams, etching on cave walls, or any electronic or mechanical methods without prior written permission from the author (except for brief quotations in the context of a raving book review, which the author eagerly welcomes).

First paperback edition August 2021

Book design by Michelle Miralles
Illustrations by Isabelle Anne M. Li

ISBN 978-1-7365254-0-1 (paperback)
ISBN 978-1-7365254-1-8 (e-book)

www.angeladfrench.com

for michelle essex

whose relentless encouragement took my writing from a far-fetched dream to the thing you now hold in your hands

CONTENTS

INTRODUCTION

JOURNEY

The dogs had been barking for weeks at all hours of the day and night. The two white terriers lived on the sixth floor of an apartment building opposite mine in a residential area of Hong Kong, and their owners often kept the windows open.

As a recent arrival in Hong Kong from the United States, I wasn't sure how to handle the situation. I could send an anonymous letter to their building. Problem: I didn't know how to write in Chinese or where to mail it. Or I could shout "shut up" in Cantonese—the primary language of Hong Kong—out my window. Problem: while I knew how to say this phrase, it would hardly be a useful way to endear myself to the neighbors.

Awaking yet again one particular dawn to the dogs' high-pitched yips and yelps, I vowed to take action. Throughout my morning ablutions, I consulted a bilingual dictionary, rehearsing what I would say to the manager of my building. I hoped he'd take pity on me and act on my behalf. When the time came, I marched up to the manager and handed him my monthly building maintenance fee as a sort of pre-complaint peace offering. As he accepted it, I barged ahead with my prepared speech in simple Cantonese.

"Sixth floor. Two dogs. I sleep!" I made sounds of barking dogs, then pointed to the next building and added, "Much trouble!"

The manager looked puzzled, so I repeated my speech with additional actions and facial expressions. "Late at night." Pointing to my watch, I offered more barking sounds. "Two. White color. Sixth floor."

The manager translated some of my Cantonese phrases to English. "Sixth floor. Noise. What time?"

With relief, I too shifted to my native tongue. "Eleven or twelve midnight."

"What noise?" he asked again.

Was he making fun of me, or did he really not understand my vocal charades?

"Dogs," I said in English, barking aloud to make sure he grasped my complaint.

A long moment of silence followed. The manager looked back and forth from the neighboring apartment building to me as if trying to decide how to deal with this foreigner and her grievance. Suddenly seeing myself through his eyes, I began to feel foolish. I'm sure I looked slightly deranged. An adult human barking like a dog is unusual in any culture, and my garbled language couldn't have improved my image. Maybe he was wondering why the authorities had granted me a Hong Kong visa in the first place.

Though we'd achieved no resolution on the matter, I finally decided we'd reached the end of our joint conversational skills—his English and my Chinese miming. With a smile and shrug, I thanked him and walked away. Who knew if the problem would be dealt with, but at least he'd have a comical story to share with his family around the dinner table that evening.

***

I grew up in central Texas in a small town near the state capital, Austin. In my childhood, the town had a population of about five thousand. My middle-class family was much like the rest of the people in our area. We dressed alike, attended the same civic and school activities, spoke in the same southern drawl, and for the most part engaged in similar pursuits and hobbies. My father is a pastor, so my childhood included being active in our church.

Very few "foreigners" came to our small town, so it was rare to meet an outsider or see a face that looked radically different from my own Caucasian features and brown hair. I do recall one exchange student from France attending my high school. When I introduced myself to her, I proudly announced, "My last name is French."

Perking up, she asked, "So what is it?"

Confused, I responded, "No, my name is French."

"Tell me how to say it," she replied.

It took a few more rounds of this Abbott and Costello-like conversation before the matter was cleared up, giving me my first encounter with cross-cultural language communication.

Music has been a part of my life for as long as I can remember. My mother began teaching me piano when I was five years old. After spending my high school years immersed in church choirs, marching band, and piano recitals, I embarked on an undergrad degree in music in another small town in Texas. Unsure what to pursue after college graduation, I did the only logical thing I could think of—went back to school and postponed living in the real world for another four years.

Midway through a dual-degree program, in which I earned a Master of Music and a Master of Divinity, I began feeling torn between a career in music and moving overseas to join some kind of Christian ministry. It's difficult to recall a time in my life when I wasn't fascinated with the concept of international and multicultural living. Throughout my childhood, I'd revered those who'd given up the comforts of home to transplant their lives to new lands. Saints who packed their belongings in a trunk, bade goodbye to their relatives, and set out on journeys of adventure and intrigue.

I still recall the stories of intrepid missionaries partaking of alligator meat, owning pet monkeys, taking jeep trips into dense jungles, or staying in bamboo huts beside snake-infested rivers. I wanted to do this. Furthermore, a few international travel experiences in my early twenties made me realize how drawn I was to living outside my home country.

At the same time, I am not a person who is comfortable with change. I dislike new situations and moving to different cities or houses. I prefer routine and the predictable. I speak no languages except English, despite a few years of high school Spanish. I require an abundance of ice in my cold drinks and am addicted to Tex-Mex food.

On the other hand, I do appreciate diversity and adventure and have a desire to see the world. I like knowing I'm part of something larger and richer than what I see around me. So, as I pondered my future, I wondered what else might be out there. Surely there were more ways of living this life than I was aware of.

Despite all the uncertainty of that time, I can now trace a clear thread of purpose that stretched from my childhood to a spring afternoon in April 2005 when I learned of a job opening in Hong Kong in the area of worship leading at an international, English-speaking church. Previously, I couldn't imagine how my varied interests in learning about other cultures, catching glimpses of the world through technology and travel, along with my innate desire to pursue music, could blend into a realistic career. But this particular opportunity seemed tailor-made for me. After consulting a world map to figure out where Hong Kong was actually located, I applied and was offered the position.

Nineteenth-century American author Mark Twain once stated:

> *Travel is fatal to prejudice, bigotry, and narrow-mindedness, and many of our people need it sorely on these accounts. Broad, wholesome, charitable views of [people] and things can not be acquired by vegetating in one little corner of the earth all one's lifetime.*[1]

Without fully understanding Twain's meaning, my desire to broaden my worldview had fueled a passion to pursue something outside myself, beyond my "little corner of the earth." So, in the summer of 2005 I moved to Hong Kong.

And my life has never been the same.

---

[1] Twain, Mark, *The Innocents Abroad* (New York: Penguin Books, 2002), 498.

CHAPTER 1

A CITY OF OPPOSITES

Landing on a Saturday morning at Hong Kong International Airport on the small man-made island of Chek Lap Kok, I was picked up by people from my new church. As we left the airport and crossed the majestic Tsing Ma suspension bridge to "Kowloon-side," my new friends explained the geography to me.

What outsiders typically refer to as Hong Kong is actually divided into three main sections: the primary island of Hong Kong, a peninsula jutting out of the Chinese Mainland called Kowloon, and the New Territories—a more rural area north of Kowloon on the Mainland. There are also 261 additional islands, mostly uninhabited and referred to as "outlying islands."

The breathtaking Victoria Harbour sits between Hong Kong Island and Kowloon. Descriptive terminology depends on the location of the speaker. If I am in another country and refer to Hong Kong, I typically mean the entire territory. When I am in the city of Hong Kong, I may reference more specifically Hong Kong-side, meaning the large island of Hong Kong, or Kowloon-side, meaning the peninsula.

The nomenclature of these sections emerged from historical events. What started out as a rural fishing village situated on the southern border of Mainland China became a British colony after the First Opium War in the 1840s. When Britain defeated China in a battle over trading rights, the Treaty of Nanjing gave Britain ownership of Hong Kong Island in perpetuity.

Following the Second Opium War in the 1850s—fought by the United Kingdom and France against China—another treaty was signed. This time the British gained control of the Kowloon Peninsula and secured command of Victoria Harbour. In 1898, Britain leased the New Territories from China for ninety-nine years. Under a third treaty, China would regain control of all three sections of the British colony of Hong Kong on July 1, 1997, known as Handover Day.

Throughout the twentieth century, thousands of people from Mainland China poured over the border into Hong Kong to escape war and poverty, particularly during World War II and the Chinese Revolution of 1949. Simultaneously, foreigners from the United Kingdom and other Western countries entered the region for business and trade, increasing the multicultural character of Hong Kong.

In the early 1980s, Hong Kongers grew increasingly anxious as they wondered how their lives would be impacted after the Handover, and many families with means and ability moved abroad. Diplomatic negotiations between British and Chinese delegations led to the 1984 signing of the Sino-British Joint Declaration. This treaty stated that Hong Kong's legal and judicial systems would remain unchanged for fifty years after the Handover, and that Hong Kong would retain a high degree of autonomy except in the areas of foreign affairs and national defense. This unique arrangement—referred to as "one country, two systems"—was fully implemented in the summer of 1997. At the end of this fifty-year transitional period, Hong Kong will be absorbed into the vast Mainland.

I'd done preliminary research on Hong Kong before my arrival, consisting mainly of perusing a National Geographic traveler's guide to the region. Hong Kong is one of the most densely populated regions on the planet with over seven million people crammed onto a relatively small plot of land. Photos revealed clusters of towering apartment buildings, numerous skyscrapers, and labyrinthine streets.

So, as we left the airport, I was surprised as I peered out the car window at the panorama of natural beauty I saw everywhere. Heavily forested mountains contrasted with sandy beaches and glittering azure seas. Despite the bustling population, I'd read that Hong Kong contains an astounding number of nature reserves, hiking trails, beaches, and other outdoor places of beauty.

Within the city, the government manages about fifteen hundred parks and gardens of various sizes. A short train or bus ride will take residents into places where only rocky crags or snaky streams and waterfalls break verdant jungles thick with elephant ears and tangled trees. My new home was definitely a city of opposites. All of which I was looking forward to exploring.

My new friends dropped me off at the flat—or, in American English, apartment—where I'd be living. I was fortunate to avoid the arduous task of apartment hunting since Hong Kong has a shortage of affordable housing, and its property market is frequently rated as the world's most expensive. My neighborhood is unique in that most residential buildings are short by Hong Kong standards—only around ten to twelve stories tall. I discovered that this was because the original Hong Kong airport had previously occupied a nearby chunk of land. Due to flight control regulations, the government had enacted height restrictions for all buildings in the area.

Compare this with most sections of Hong Kong where residential buildings tower over the streets with fifty to sixty floors or more. No other city in the world has as many skyscrapers. In fact, Hong Kong has been referred to as the world's tallest city, reflecting the percentage of its residents who live high up in so-called pencil towers—thin structures that soar skyward while occupying a small footprint of land.

I also quickly learned that my particular apartment building sits in the shadow of the famed Lion Rock, so named because its contour looks vaguely like a lion's profile when viewed from certain angles. Standing between Kowloon and the New Territories, Lion Rock provides some of the best hikes and lookout points in the city. Taking a cue from the landmark, Hong Kongers have adopted what they call the "Lion Rock spirit," a phrase that references the "can-do" attitude that characterizes so many of its citizens.

Until arriving in Hong Kong, I had never lived in a large city. Even the Texas towns in which my college and graduate school were located seemed relatively small. I couldn't yet envision myself living in such an urban environment. How long would it take me to get familiar with day-to-day living here?

Still, though overwhelmingly huge, this new city also felt exciting and vibrant. I began thinking of the multitude of opportunities ahead of me. All the new and different experiences I could anticipate. The exhilaration of meeting people from all over the world.

And thus began my life in Hong Kong.

CHAPTER 2

M*A*S*H AND COCA-COLA

Exploring my new home became my first adventure. I'm still not certain who made the interior design decisions, but my flat came with unusual features. The walls were pale-pink. Each light-switch cover was a different color—two pale-green, one dark-blue, one black, a baby-blue, a neon-orange, and a few white ones with various silver or gold stripes. The entire floor consisted of light-brown wood laminate except for a single blue-and-green square in the entryway and three colored stripes of blue, green, and burgundy in the hallway.

A similar oddity could be seen in the kitchen. Amidst floor-to-ceiling white tiles were two randomly-placed decorative tiles. One depicted a scene of an antique wood stove, the other a rustic fireplace. Both were charming but out of character with the ultra-modern purple and gray cabinetry.

Previous tenants had left various articles of decor, kitchen utensils, linens, and other odds and ends. The flat had also served as a repository of unwanted giveaway furniture. Grateful though

I was to move into a fully furnished flat, I was a bit puzzled by the hodgepodge. Throughout those first few months, I took time to methodically sort through drawers, cabinets, and closets to ascertain what I had.

This included three can-openers, two kitchen timers shaped like tomatoes, keys to doors or locks that no longer existed, and sheets for ten to twelve beds. Many of the linens looked hand-stitched from the 1950s. There were also books in an assortment of languages I neither spoke nor read, and several sets of stereo speakers without a stereo. There were enough mismatched plates and glasses to serve a multitude, along with four baking dishes, though only one would fit in the tiny oven.

The living-room was filled with wall-to-wall furniture—literally. I could barely squeeze around the coffee table that was situated between the sofa and entertainment center. Amusingly, in the latter were seventeen VCR tapes filled with old *M*A*S*H* episodes.

Each day brought a new and interesting find, like an ongoing treasure hunt. A full set of ornate gilded china nestled in a bedside bureau in the master bedroom. A 1970s-orange crock-pot was in the other bedside bureau. Spare light bulbs for the bedrooms filled bathroom shelves, while a bottle of metal pot cleaner resided in a bedroom drawer. A can of tomato soup was so ancient I dropped it in the rubbish bin. Finding a lovely candleholder in a closet, I moved it to a more prominent place.

My new mantra regarding the mismatch of furnishings became a nonchalant, "It was like that when I moved here."

When visiting friends asked why I had four spatulas and no large cooking spoon, I shrugged. "It was like that when I moved here."

Other visitors questioned, "Why does that bookcase have a slanted top shelf? And what's the deal with an electrical outlet located up by the ceiling on the living-room wall?"

Another shrug. "I don't know. It was like that when I moved in."

***

It took some time and effort to make this interestingly furnished flat my own. But I grew to love my fortress of solitude, and I relished a sense of comfort and contentment. Except when my downstairs neighbor rang my doorbell at 7:00 a.m. one morning to complain that her ceiling was caving in because my bathtub was leaking.

At least she spoke a little English. Within days of moving to Hong Kong, I'd felt humbled by the sheer number of residents who spoke two, three, four, or even more languages fluently. The official languages of Hong Kong are Chinese and English. This is confusing because the term Chinese refers to both ethnicity and the written language, but the most prevalent *spoken* language is Cantonese, which is also utilized in a few southern provinces of Mainland China.

Cantonese has completely different pronunciations than Mandarin, the primary language of Mainland China (where Mandarin is referred to as *Putonghua*). As an expat learning the language, I was baffled by the fact that written characters are the same for both Cantonese and Mandarin, but spoken words sound completely dissimilar. Further complicating the matter, there are two forms of written Chinese—traditional, which is used in Hong Kong and Taiwan, and simplified, which is employed in the Mainland. Essentially, reading and speaking are two distinct systems.

Because of the historic influence of the British, English is widely used within the Hong Kong government and by legal and business sectors. Most professionals speak both Cantonese and Mandarin, as well as English, which facilitates cross-border and international business. Added in are other immigrant groups like Filipinos and Indonesians, who not only speak multiple dialects from their home countries but are already fluent in English and quickly pick up Cantonese.

I took Cantonese lessons throughout the first year I lived in Hong Kong, yet very little stayed in my brain. My feeble excuse is that locals—noticing my Caucasian features—immediately switch to English, so I am not forced to practice Cantonese. Although there are several versions of *pinyin*, a system that transcribes Chinese characters into romanized letters so foreigners can learn to pronounce words, I can't read the Chinese characters. And since these characters don't dictate sounds, it's impossible to pick up the spoken language by reading or looking at signs and advertisements.

Most challenging for me, Cantonese and Mandarin are both tonal languages, so one syllable can have different meanings depending on the pitch with which it's spoken. This often gets me into trouble. My language blunders have been numerous as I've stumbled through the sounds and tones of Cantonese, many of which have left my friends and neighbors reeling with laughter.

One morning soon after arriving in Hong Kong, I exited my building. There I encountered a management worker from my apartment complex watering the plants. Feeling overconfident, I asked in Cantonese, "Do you like to water the plants?"

Except what I actually said was, "Do you like to *wash* the plants?"

A few weeks later, I commented on the weather—or so I thought—to another worker from my building. Pointing toward the sky, I said a word I thought meant "rain." Unfortunately, the word that emerged was actually the Cantonese translation of "Coca-Cola." Which made me sound like a thirsty lunatic with a sweet tooth.

My most frequent language struggle though is a complete lack of vocabulary. I spout a few phrases or words to a Cantonese-speaking local, then stand gape-mouthed as the other person, assuming (wrongly) that I must be fluent, replies with a flurry of responses. The truth is that I'm more like a highly trained parrot. I can repeat what I hear, but the comprehension or ability to carry on a conversation is largely absent. To quote a Hong Kong octogenarian English student I know: "Sometimes my head is empty."

A brilliant depiction of such moments.

CHAPTER 3

OCTOPI AND RATTLETRAPS

Since I didn't drive in Hong Kong, I was grateful to discover I could easily walk the distance between my home and work, and between my home and several shopping centers. With on-foot as my primary mode of mobility, it became apparent early on that I needed all kinds of bags to haul groceries, umbrellas, books, and other belongings from one place to another. These included backpacks, shopping sacks, Christmas gift bags, voluminous purses, luggage trolleys, and rolling suitcases. I had to get creative, based on what I could lift or carry and how far I needed to travel.

This was the kind of everyday living challenge not covered in Hong Kong guidebooks, and no research materials I'd read before moving to the city prepared me for such awkward situations. For instance, how to deliver a homemade cake to a colleague. Or how to bring a hot pan of green beans to a potluck gathering. Or how to step into a double-decker bus with a case of soda under one arm and a twelve-count package of toilet paper under the other without knocking out the elderly passengers around me.

Life grew easier with each passing week as I adjusted to carrying only what I needed for that day while leaving the rest at home. The short trek from my flat to my office became a routine, and I started noticing the same familiar faces each day. The most recognizable were those who worked in my apartment complex: the manager, the caretaker, and three guards.

The caretaker, a bright-eyed woman with straggly gray hair, always wore black Capri pants and the same flowered blouse. She greeted me cheerfully each time we encountered one another. But I had the sense she was studying me, trying to figure out why I do what I do. And why I generated so much trash.

My favorite guard was a woman who had tossed aside the inscrutable face I'd come to expect from Hong Kongers. She greeted me and other building residents with great enthusiasm, huge smiles, and friendly laughs. She admired babies and children, waved hello and goodbye to people of all ages, and made cheerful comments about the weather. Sometimes she asked if I was going to church, her question accompanied by making the sign of the cross. I would nod and smile. It seemed everyone employed in the building knew I worked in a church, so this became a common question.

Another guard, visibly missing a few teeth, habitually waved to me while uttering the same English phrase in a singsong voice: "Gud mawning!" His wave was peculiar with the arm extended and palm angled out and down. No wrist or elbow movement, just a stiff, slow back-and-forth as though he was standing on a high balcony waving to a crowd below. This guard frequently offered me a cigarette or a bite of his dinner. I never understood if this was a joke or not, but I declined both with a polite smile and quickly moved along.

***

On days when I needed to run errands or travel beyond walking distance, I climbed aboard a minibus, which took me to the nearby train station. But to do this, I first needed to procure an Octopus card. Introduced in the late 1990s, the Octopus card is one of the cleverest features of Hong Kong technology and a versatile tool in the local transportation system. It took me awhile to sort out the reason for its name, but I was fascinated by what I learned.

The Octopus card has distinct English and Cantonese appellations. In Cantonese, it is known as *baat daaht tung*, which roughly translates as "eight arrived pass" or "go everywhere pass." The number eight in the Cantonese name links it to the English name of the card, Octopus, a sea creature which of course has eight tentacles. The intent is to suggest a creature with appendages reaching out toward all sections of the city. The number eight is an added bonus as it represents good luck in Chinese culture. The card displays an infinity symbol logo, which also doubles as a figure eight.

This all-in-one smartcard can be pre-loaded with money for riding on buses, trains, ferries, trams, and other transportation systems as well as to pay for metered or garage parking and tunnel tolls. It can also be used to purchase items from vending machines, 7-Eleven and Circle-K stores, the post office, fast-food restaurants, coffee shops, and supermarkets. Likewise entry fees to swimming pools, movie theaters, and more.

The card also functions as an ID at times. Students may scan their cards to record attendance or access library materials at school. Residents of certain apartment complexes or workers in commercial buildings use their card for entry. Banks can link the Octopus card to an account and automatically top up the balance when it drops below a specific threshold. Cards can also be refilled at supermarkets, convenience stores, and train station kiosks.

The Octopus card company sells other products with embedded chips linked to an account such as watches, key chains, cell phone cases, and other trinkets, meaning that many people don't even carry the actual card. Not that toting around the card is a problem, as it can be scanned through wallets and purses, eliminating the need to pull it out. Around ninety-nine percent of the city's population utilizes the Octopus cards. The entire system has won numerous awards and has been copied by public transport systems in other countries.

In short, the Octopus card embodies much of what Hong Kong is best known for: cutting edge technology, a fast-paced and on-the-go lifestyle, convenience, and efficiency. Also seafood.

***

After work one day, I needed to do some errands, so I decided to take the minibus. It was pouring rain. I had a book-bag over one shoulder, a sack of groceries on my arm, and an open umbrella in one hand. The sixteen-passenger minibus I hailed screeched to a halt a few feet from the curb, and I began to climb the steep stairs into the bus.

All the while, I attempted to close my umbrella, locate my Octopus card, and try to keep myself from getting drenched by the rain. The minibus driver cursed and threatened to pull away from the curb before I could get both feet in the vehicle. As the bus took off, I lurched into a seat, dropped my sopping umbrella to the floor, and clutched at my bags to keep them from falling on a seatmate, who peered at me cautiously. During the wild ride, I clung to handrails and the seat in front of me while digging my feet into the floor. Without an adequate sense of balance, I might have fallen out of my seat into the aisle—and, in fact, did on other occasions.

A sign noting the maximum allowed speed of the minibus was displayed next to a huge digital speedometer. This clearly wasn't meant to be taken seriously since the bus careened around corners, seemingly on two wheels, starting and stopping with alarming abruptness. As if in a race, the driver wove through traffic, cut into queues at stoplights, hopped the curbs on tight turns, and generally created a partly-thrilling, partly-horrifying experience for the passengers.

The brakes squealed like a terrified guinea pig while every inch of the aging vehicle rattled, vibrated, shook, and clattered. As we rounded a corner, I imagined a wheel flying off—like in a cartoon—and the entire bus collapsing into a heap of doors and windows, a puff of smoke lazily rising from the wreckage.

We were now nearing my destination. I shouted out the name of my stop to the driver. My newly-acquired Cantonese competed with the radio, seatmates chatting on mobile phones, and the general cacophony of the rattletrap, so I couldn't be sure the driver had heard me. But with screeching brakes, the bus began to slow.

The driver pulled a lever, and the metal folding door slammed open. I stumbled toward the exit, stepping over other passengers and their belongings. Grabbing the handrails, I descended the steps. My bags were barely clear of the door and my legs on solid ground when the bus whipped away from the curb.

At least the wild ride had a happy ending. Thankfully, in the ensuing years transport companies began replacing these older minibuses. The new vehicles also contain seatbelts, which I should probably utilize.

* * *

When I wasn't focusing on preserving my life, I found great amusement in studying the dashboard and driver's area of the various minibuses in which I rode. Like a clerk who works at a desk in an office, these drivers amassed their belongings around them in a homely fashion. In just one such vehicle, a calendar hung from the air conditioning vent, secured with a twisty tie. A diminutive vase of water affixed to the dash held a live and growing bamboo shoot. The driver's own water bottle sat in a cupholder fashioned from recycled cardboard and plastic ties. An empty cigarette carton duct-taped to the dashboard held a mobile phone.

Washcloths and cleaning utensils hung on the bar separating the driver's seat from passenger seats. Spare umbrellas leaned in the corner, while a neatly folded newspaper lay nearby. A plastic bin jury-rigged onto the engine cover was filled with the driver's reading material, lunch box, jacket, and other personal belongings. A broken sun-visor was held up by a chip clip attached to some string, which was attached to a key ring, which was attached to a screw, which was attached to the ceiling of the bus. Minibuses appeared to be a good place to exercise skills in resourcefulness.

Home sweet clattering home.

CHAPTER 4

UMBRELLAS AND CRYING WALLS

After the minibus experience, I undertook the learning of other public transportation systems in Hong Kong, which are world-class and user-friendly. This city has mastered the art of keeping a vast network of trains, subways, buses, trams, ferries, light-rails, and taxis running smoothly, efficiently, and cheaply. They're very clean too.

On a Saturday evening the second or third weekend after I moved to Hong Kong, I rode the MTR (Mass Transit Railway) to the home of new friends. I noticed right away that the MTR system map, organization, and labeling are brilliantly simple and easy to navigate. Both visual and audio announcements notify passengers of relevant information. A recording of a woman with a delightful British accent calls out the approaching station names in Cantonese, Mandarin, and English. This voice is not computer generated but a real person named Cheri. My favorite recording, which I only hear on certain sections of a particular line, poetically says, "Please alight on the right."

Cheri also conveys warnings around the escalators inside the stations. When a train arrives and people disembark, a crush of humanity tries to merge onto the few narrow escalators. People journeying with rolling suitcases, carts, or strollers are encouraged to use the elevator to prevent people tripping over them on the fast-moving escalators. Cheri's disembodied voice on the traveling stairway warns, "Please hold the handrail. Don't keep your eyes only on your mobile phone."

Most train lines on the MTR are located underground, though some sections emerge aboveground in rural areas. By some incredible feat of engineering I'll never understand, the train runs under the harbor—a fact I try not to think about when hurtling through a sub-oceanic channel encased in a metal carriage. In fact, there are numerous tunnels around this hilly seaside city carrying automobiles, buses, and trains through mountains and under water.

That Saturday evening, despite new trains arriving every two to three minutes, hundreds of other passengers and I waited in a queue to get to the train door. Shuffling in a slow-moving line with people pushing from behind—albeit gently—brought on feelings of claustrophobia. As I stepped into the train car, people pressed against me on all sides until I was literally rubbing shoulders with strangers. Trying to read a book or look at my phone would be futile since my elbows were scrunched so tightly against my body I couldn't even move my arms.

Instead, I closed my eyes and grabbed for a handrail or strap, an unnecessary precaution because if the train lurched, I'd have nowhere to fall. Simultaneously, I attempted to avoid smelling the armpit of whoever was squashed against me clinging to the same overhead strap. I feared missing my stop due to the crowd blocking the door. So when the train finally pulled into my station, I had to be pushy and assertive just to exit the carriage.

I avoided taking the MTR on Saturday evenings for several months after that experience. But in time I realized that the train was an enjoyable mode of transportation at non-peak hours. The subway cars had excellent air conditioning, and of all the options in Hong Kong, this form of travel caused me the least amount of motion sickness. With Hong Kong's subtropical heat and the human propensity to sweat, early morning train rides proved far more aromatically pleasant than crowded evening rush-hour rides.

***

I'd arrived in Hong Kong during the month of August, the wettest month of the year for the region. Getting around a crowded city already presented challenges, and I learned quickly that rain complicated all forms of Hong Kong transportation. Venturing into the elements without an umbrella was unthinkable, and—awkward though they were—the jumbo umbrellas were more likely to function properly in the wind. I also learned firsthand that, just as in movies and comics, a bus racing past really did send a muddied spray of water at the innocent pedestrian on the sidewalk—i.e., me.

People carry umbrellas everywhere in Hong Kong, not just for rain but also in bright daylight to protect skin from the sun. The devices come in all sizes, shapes, and colors. They may be swathed in polka dots, flowers, or butterfly-covered purple nylon. Some display advertising for companies or businesses such as the bright orange, green, and white stripes of 7-Eleven. Other canopies may depict nature scenes, cartoon characters, animal patterns, or solid hues. Kids' parasols may be topped with Mickey Mouse ears, frogs' eyes, or other 3-D figures. Rubber tips added to the end aid the elderly in walking.

Umbrellas are available for sale in shops, sidewalk kiosks, department stores, convenience stores, and even vending machines in train stations. Plastic-sleeve dispensers are situated at the entrance of malls and shopping centers so customers can wrap their wet parasol to keep the floors dry. Buckets, bins, and umbrella holders of all sizes and shapes stand inside doorways. Deposit your dripping canopy as you enter and retrieve it when you depart later.

A few weeks after my move to Hong Kong, I ventured out on a rainy day to meet new friends at a local restaurant that had such a bin by the door. I thoughtlessly dropped my umbrella in the bucket, then walked over to our table to enjoy lunch, a meal that included my first taste of chicken feet.

Exiting the restaurant later, I realized I had no idea which umbrella was mine. Like so much else, my umbrella had come from my flat, left there by previous tenants. I'd never looked at it closely. With much trepidation, I chose one from the bucket I thought *could* be mine. As I slipped out the door, I wondered what level of offense umbrella theft constituted, and hoped I wouldn't be deported for an unintentional crime so early in my Hong Kong tenure.

Then I went home and tied a colorful bit of ribbon to the handles of all my umbrellas.

* * *

One aspect of Hong Kong I noticed immediately upon arrival—and to which I've never adjusted even after living in the city many years—is the heat and humidity. For most of the year, I walk around dripping with sweat, clothes drenched, hair wet and stringy, mopping my face with tissues. I look like a drowned rat. People say that long-term exposure to humidity is good for the complexion. I say that a drowned rat with nice skin is still a drowned rat.

A look at Hong Kong's weather forecast doesn't adequately convey the misery of its humidity. With average lows and highs around 62°F and 86°F (17°C and 30°C respectively), it sounds mild and pleasant. But dampness exacerbates the temperatures, making the hot feel hotter and the cold feel colder. I've experienced some of the most extreme temperatures of my life in Hong Kong. There's something about the mugginess that creeps into the body, seeps out of the pores, and makes life torturous, outdoors and indoors, summer and winter.

In the summer months when relative humidity is around eighty percent, the heat index skyrockets to wretchedness. I run my window-unit air-conditioners when I'm home and hope the place doesn't melt when they are switched off while I'm out during the day. The record high I've logged inside my flat is 90.5° F (32.5° C).

I soon learned that in the early spring months when the weather suddenly warms up after a cool spell, moisture forms on indoor concrete floors, walls, and ceilings. It looks like someone has come through with a mop or spray bottle. Hence, the local idiom: "the walls are crying." Sometimes I, too, cry in response to the miserable weather. Or maybe it's just sweat on my face.

In Hong Kong, it's so humid that bath towels are perpetually damp with a sour, musty smell. Bread left in its original wrapping on the counter molds in two days or less. Fruit and other perishables quickly spoil outside the refrigerator. Concrete walls wrinkle and bubble around the window due to moisture seeping in from the sills.

It's so humid that batteries corrode inside electronics, remote controls, and clocks. Books, papers, and photos grow damp and moldy. Supermarkets devote entire aisles to moisture-reducing products such as electric dehumidifiers and giant versions of those non-edible desiccant packets found inside medication bottles. In this mammoth form, they are designed to be placed in closets and cabinets to pull water from the air.

It's so humid that unused envelopes that have been sitting in a drawer are already sealed shut. Same problem with postage stamps. An acoustic piano or guitar must be purchased locally rather than shipped from abroad, as the wood in Hong Kong is specially treated to withstand damp conditions.

I gave up on washing sweaters by hand. If it's going to take over a week to dry, I'd rather send it to the cleaners. My preparation for baking includes hacking away at formerly granulated sugar with a strong knife. Double-walled "sweat-proof" drinking cups have moisture trapped between the layers as well as condensation on the outside. Apparently the manufacturing company didn't test their products near the equator.

It's so humid in Hong Kong that people routinely say: "Don't take a deep breath outside or you'll drown!"

CHAPTER 5

BOUNCY CASTLES AND DURIAN

Due to high temperatures and humidity coupled with weak arms that grew tired of schlepping groceries home, I began utilizing taxis more often. While mass transport was more economical and environmentally friendly, I'd already knocked out too many people on the minibus when hauling bulky bags. The limbs and lives of fellow passengers were worth the extra cost.

One adjustment I made when grocery shopping was to calculate the weight of items in my cart as well as the price. When not taking a taxi or bus, my trek home included a fifteen-minute walk, a hike from the street to my building, and an elevator ride up to my floor. It occurred to me this was why my neighbors did small daily shopping rather than purchasing a week's worth of food at once. For the same reason, I quickly kicked a diet soda addiction, switching to iced tea for my caffeine needs. Approximate weight of one can of soft drink: 340 grams. Approximate weight of a box of one hundred tea bags: 200 grams.

Many of my early taxi experiences reminded me of driving a theme park go-cart. The steering wheel seemed disconnected from the axle so that the vehicle fishtailed easily. With too much play in the wheel, the driver had difficulty making small adjustments to the car's direction. The result for me was an immediate onset of motion sickness. Other taxi rides felt as if the driver had one foot each on the gas and brake, resulting in constant jerking as he alternated between pedals.

Cab drivers work long shifts, which causes the seat springs to wear out over time. On one such ride, I had the sensation of plopping down on a kid's air-filled bouncy castle. Bumps in the road became thrill-inducing vaults into the air, my head coming dangerously close to the ceiling, followed by a double-bounce landing on aged vinyl.

On other occasions, I found myself in taxis with particularly chatty drivers who wanted to converse either in English (to expand their own vocabulary) or Cantonese (to test the limits of mine). After determining my destination and route, they typically asked the same questions. Do you speak Cantonese? Where are you from? How long have you lived in Hong Kong? What do you think of Hong Kong? What do you think of [insert name of current American president]?

One time a cab driver asked if I'd write the English word "beautiful" in his little notebook. Perhaps he was planning ahead for a date that night and wanted to impress a good-looking girl.

In Hong Kong, it's illegal to talk on a hand-held cell phone while driving, but hands-free talking is allowed. Since cab drivers participate in multiple ride arrangement services, they often have several mobile phones, usually connected to the car engine for power. I sat in one taxi where the driver operated eight phones, all lined up on the dashboard with a tangled mass of wires running behind the steering wheel. I have no idea how he kept up with all the numbers and phones since the average human head is limited to just two ears.

* * *

During my first months of living in Hong Kong until I settled into my new Asian life, I found it easier to frequent a Western supermarket that sold products familiar to me and that I knew how to prepare. The grocery store I chose had few roasted geese hanging in the window, and I could always locate crunchy peanut butter, cereal, Oreos, and other necessities.

This store was located in a mall that used a bizarre system of floor numbering. From bottom to top, they were labeled LG2, LG1, G, UG, L1 and L2. The UG stood for upper ground, but I mistakenly thought of it as underground. The LG referred to lower ground, while L1 was level one. Thus the L had two different meanings within the same building.

One of my Hong Kong Chinese friends remarked with exasperation, "The floors in this shopping center were named by the British!"

The employees who stocked the shelves of this Western supermarket were clearly less familiar with imported food items, as they sometimes wrongly categorized products. Mayonnaise was located next to spaghetti sauce, oyster sauce, curry, and tortillas. Cornmeal sat next to the rice, rather than with flour and other baking ingredients. Nestled among cake and cookie mixes, I found a box of instant scalloped potatoes—a legitimate mistake since Betty Crocker manufactured both the spuds and the desserts.

On one occasion, I inadvertently purchased a can of cherries instead of kidney beans since they sat side-by-side on the shelf. This was entirely my fault for not reading the English label or looking closely at the picture.

At first I tried inquiring about products I couldn't find, using a limited English vocabulary and a bit of miming. But playing charades in an attempt to locate hamburger buns or ground cloves proved futile. Other times, I blindly made decisions without asking for help. In one disappointing circumstance, I learned there exists a significant difference between green onions and leeks.

On another occasion, I studied a package of leafy greens to determine what plant it was. The label was unhelpful. Its English wording read: "A vegetable." Amusingly, I learned years later this was actually local slang for the plant in question. It is similar to Romaine lettuce, and because of the vague A-shape of the raw leaves, it's called "A vegetable."

It should be noted that most of the anecdotes described here occurred prior to the advent of smartphones with Googling capability. Since then, my life has grown increasingly dull. Now when I need to purchase an obscure product, I conduct a quick image search on my phone, show a picture to the shopkeeper, and successfully depart with my items.

While exploring groceries, I noticed a trend in which supermarkets sold products that resembled Western foodstuffs, but which were indigenous in style and flavor. Oatmeal and other hot cereals came in flavors such as chicken, pork, or shrimp. Potato chips with uncommon seasonings were available in abundance: seaweed, roasted ox, honey soy chicken, cream of mushroom soup, shrimp, wasabi, pea, honey butter, salmon sushi, lobster bisque, sour plum, dill pickle, curry, and crispy goose liver.

The fresh produce section of grocery stores offered a considerable collection. Vegetables included *choi sum, bak choi*, multiple types of Asian kale, lettuces, and many other greens for which I didn't yet know the correct terminology. And I had no idea there existed so many different kinds of mushrooms. In the fruit section, I found dragon fruit, kumquat, Buddhist melon, persimmon, durian, star fruit, lychee, mangosteen, jackfruit, pomelo, and rambutan—all with tastes as exotic as their names. New friends were eager to share these delicacies with me, and I enjoyed tasting them despite some of them resembling alien life forms.

Durian was the single exception. I'd never heard of the fruit before moving to Hong Kong. Its smell is so off-putting I've never dared to taste it. Due to its pungent odor, durian is frequently prohibited in hotels, airplanes, public transport, and even some supermarkets. One author described it this way:

> *The durian, which resembles a pineapple crossed with an armadillo, has a teeth-chattering sweetness... [But] it is the aroma one never forgets. The best description I have heard of it—from a Singapore hotelier who refuses to allow it on his premises—is "one ton of overripe Limburger cheese, only more so."*[2]

I'm given to understand the enjoyment of durian is an acquired taste. Which begs the question: what person in history took notice of this unsightly, malodorous fruit and said, "Let's give this a try!"

One day soon after arriving in Hong Kong, I was on a hunt for a tub of chocolate frosting. I wandered around the supermarket for several minutes, looking at shelves of baking ingredients, before mustering the courage to ask an employee. When I pointed to a

---

[2] Anson, Robert Sam, "Sixth Sense," in *Traveler's Tales: Thailand*, eds. O'Reilly, James and Larry Habegger (San Francisco: Traveler's Tales, 1993), 7-8.

picture on a cake mix box, his eyes lit up with comprehension. Guiding me to the next aisle, he proudly offered me a can of Hershey's chocolate syrup. I didn't have the heart to point out his mistake, so I smiled, thanked him, and purchased the syrup anyway. That poor young man would be forever confused about Western desserts while I enjoyed an unexpected glass of chocolate milk.

A few weeks later, a new friend took me shopping at a wet market, a cheaper venue for purchasing unprocessed food. In Hong Kong, these kinds of markets are usually situated inside a building with stalls and booths that sell fresh fruit and vegetables, live seafood, butchered meat, and other perishables. The concrete floor is often wet due to sea creatures splashing in vats of water or shopkeepers hosing off the refuse from meat slaughtering. Hence the name "wet market."

In the past, shopkeepers sold live chickens in these markets. But government regulators began to limit this practice as the threat of avian flu increased. I've been told that many Hong Kongers prefer to see their food while still alive to ensure its quality and freshness.

Hong Kong is a city of contradictions in the sense that the real and the fake stand side-by-side. The authenticity of food, particularly meat, is of utmost importance to Hong Kongers. Whole cooked chickens, ducks, and geese hang in the windows of restaurants. Large portions of pork or beef suspend from meat hooks at butcher shops. Poultry is always served on the bone, and seafood is brought to the table with all its outer parts still intact. Diners and grocery shoppers want to know that they are eating fresh, genuine meat, rather than processed food with unknown substances added.

Yet Asia is notorious for making knock-off goods available to the general public. A stroll through Hong Kong street markets is accompanied by the singsong chorus of "copy watch, copy handbag" echoing from the lips of enterprising shop owners, even though this kind of business is discouraged in the city.

Authentic meat and knock-off handbags. Diversity and paradox are what make this city fascinating and yet almost unknowable. Martin Burnett, in his history of the Hong Kong tram system, says it this way:

> *Unlike other cosmopolitan cities, however, Hong Kong cannot be called a melting pot. The different streams of life mingle here but they do not mix; they prefer to live alongside each other.*[3]

The real and the fake. Old and new. Traditional and modern. East and West. That's Hong Kong as I was growing in my understanding of it.

***

A classic example of West meets East is the double-decker bus, which comes straight from the streets of London. Not long after arriving in Hong Kong, I took the opportunity to experience one. I chose the front seat of the top deck, generally referred to as the "suicide seat" by locals. I learned the reasons for that nickname as I found myself instinctively ducking when overhanging tree branches whipped the windshield, and my heart stopped beating when the bus braked mere centimeters from the vehicle in front of it.

---

[3] Barnett, Martin, *Tramlines: The Story of the Hong Kong Tramway System* (Hong Kong: South China Morning Post, Ltd., 1984), 7.

For me though, it was a huge picture window for unobstructed sightseeing as the double-deckers offered views not available in other vehicles. From above, throngs of pedestrians crossing the streets looked like—well, throngs of pedestrians. But the sheer number of human beings out on the sidewalks was not as obvious when I was threading my way among them.

Dark heads. Colorful handbags and jackets. A sea of round umbrella tops. A straggler rushing through the crosswalk on a red light. Peeks into second floor shops. Close-ups of rusted neon signs and leaky air conditioners. Looking into apartment windows. Watching laundry flap in the wind. Making eye-contact with passengers of adjacent double-decker buses. These were all vignettes of Hong Kong life from a different perspective.

The climb to and from the upper deck was an adventure in itself, as I maneuvered the narrow, steep staircase while avoiding other riders and frantically grasping at handrails because the vehicle was moving. On one particular double-decker ride, the bus lurched unexpectedly while I hurried up the steps. I was thankful my friend was in front of me, rather than a stranger, because I suddenly planted my face in her calves.

And that illustrates why I so often take a taxi home after shopping for groceries. My friend on the staircase would not have appreciated me slamming into her legs with a six-pack of diet soda and a can of Hershey's syrup.

Let it be known that I later learned how to make homemade chocolate frosting.

CHAPTER 6

PIG KNUCKLES AND CHOPSTICKS

Over the first few months in Hong Kong, as people introduced me to their favorite restaurants, I experienced a wide variety of meals. I began to adjust to the ritual of dining on Chinese food—which is, of course, nothing like American-style Chinese food.

No matter the occasion or company, a typical Hong Kong dinner generally occurred in similar fashion. A family would invite me out to eat, and we would patronize a nearby eatery. We'd be seated at a round table in a jam-packed, low-ceilinged room. Studying the Chinese-language menu, my hosts would announce that we'd be partaking of "ordinary dishes" as opposed to *dim sum* or hot pot.

Dim sum, the cuisine Hong Kong is best known for, is a style of eating that consists of an assortment of dumplings and buns, most steamed with shrimp, vegetables, pork, or other meat as filling. Additional bite-sized items can also be ordered, such as spring rolls, beef balls, chicken feet, or glutinous rice dumplings. The servings are small, and usually three or four portions are brought to the table in a steaming bamboo basket.

There is no particular sequence for this meal, which is typically eaten in the morning or at lunchtime, rarely for dinner. Each item is shared and consumed when it arrives at the table, while still fresh and hot. Dim sum is best experienced with a large group, since more people at a table means a greater variety of dishes can be ordered and sampled.

In wintery months, a favorite Hong Kong cuisine is hot pot. A proper hot pot restaurant has tables designed for this style of eating with a central built-in cauldron and heat source so everyone has easy access to the pot. This boiling vat is divided into two sections, each filled with a different soup base. Typically, one is bland broth and the other a spicier option. Diners order seafood, meat, and vegetables, which are served raw and thinly sliced.

Everyone proceeds to cook their own meal by dropping the ingredients into the boiling liquid. Chopsticks can be used to hold a bit of shaved beef in the broth, or soup with cooked veggies can be ladled into a bowl.

Hot pot is a steaming, time-consuming meal best enjoyed in cold weather with a group of friends. Although delicious, it's not my favorite style of eating. I'm happy to allow someone else to cook my food.

In contrast, a meal of "ordinary dishes" involves a variety of food available on the menu. My hosts will ask me what I like or dislike, then begin ordering a balanced meal to be shared by all at the table.

"Do you like seafood?" they query.

This is a complicated question. I love eating seafood in the United States. But to a person who grew up in Central Texas, far from the coast, seafood connotes images of succulent shrimp, already peeled and beheaded, or deep-fried, deboned fish fillets without the fins or head. Or even the British classic: fried fish and chips.

In Asia, seafood refers to any creature found in any body of water. Peculiar-looking shellfish. Aromatic scallops. Shrimp bits. Eel nuggets. Squid rings. Frog pieces. Rubbery octopus. Not to mention plenty of other marine life for which I don't even know the English terminology.

Other types of meat on the menu may include tripe, pig knuckles (I never knew swine had flexible appendages), cow stomach, various animal intestinal parts, oxtail and ox tongue (both ends available for consumption; I think the tail tastes better). There are also chicken feet, duck, goose, and other fowl (head and beak included), and so forth. Hong Kongers can never be accused of food wastefulness. They utilize every part of the creature.

The Cantonese-style roasted chicken is one of my favorite local dishes. Succulent and flavorful, the whole chicken is laid out and chopped into segments with a giant cleaver, then served on a large platter—head, skin, and bones included. This means each piece of chicken has bone fragments and visible bone marrow around which the eater must maneuver. Nevertheless, delicious.

Next, my local friends and I discuss veggies. Sometimes my host can't remember the exact English translation. At other times there is no English equivalent, so they describe how it grows, its color, shape, size, etc. Green vegetables are bountiful in this part of the world, and I'm always thankful for the consistent, dependable taste of fiber in the midst of an otherwise unpredictable meal. You can't go wrong with a vegetable pan-fried in oil and topped with generous portions of minced garlic.

Rice and noodles are a must at almost any meal and are usually mouthwateringly good. But watch out: you never know what might be mixed in with the noodles or hiding under a clump of rice. That tripe always finds its way into the meal somehow.

Once we've ordered the food, the dishes need to be properly "washed." This procedure begins by pouring boiling water or tea from a teapot into each bowl, cup, and plate, then dipping spoons, chopsticks, and any other utensils therein. Apparently diners feel they can't trust the kitchen staff to carry out their job adequately. Once rinsed, we pour the soiled water into a large bowl, which the waiter removes.

Thanks to a Korean roommate in college, I moved to Hong Kong with basic chopstick skills. But I quickly learned that a Chinese-style spoon must be utilized along with the chopsticks to convey soup and noodles to the mouth. Or to help get that hard-to-grasp spring roll onto my tongue and not into my teacup.

I began to notice that Hong Kong people eating in Western restaurants—i.e., with knife and fork—employ the two-handed approach, holding the knife with the dominant hand and the fork in the other. I grew up using the "cut-and-switch" method, which means picking up the knife to cut a bit of food while holding the fork with the non-dominant hand, then setting the knife down and swapping the fork back to the dominant hand.

I've tried to convert to the more efficient two-handed way, but I struggle with holding a fork upside down (British-style) when putting a bite into my mouth. I end up with odd combinations of various styles—all impolite no matter the country. As evidenced on one occasion when I ate dinner with my family back in the United States and noticed my sister eyeing me curiously. Following her gaze to my plate, I discovered I was inexplicably holding two forks, one in each hand.

When the "ordinary dishes" arrive—one at a time, and in no particular order—at the meal with my Hong Kong friends, we first take the obligatory photos of the people gathered and food displayed. This practice is so prevalent that a local idiom says, "The camera eats first."

All food is shared by all diners at the table, regardless of who ordered what. Members of our party might take personal offense if I decline a particular dish or fail to eat ample amounts of the feast. Moreover, those on either side of me or anyone within a chopstick's reach routinely place food in my bowl without regard for my polite refusals or adamant protests.

Napkins aren't offered, though a box of papery-thin tissue will be placed on the table. I learned early on to follow the example of locals by carrying a Kleenex packet with me for such occasions, though Hong Kongers are astonishingly neat in their eating habits. I'm the one who needs something to wipe my grease-laden chin or clean up the large percentage of my meal that fell off my chopsticks.

At least two teapots are also present on the table, one containing strong tea, the other boiling water. Diners get refills of either or both in any amount or succession. I was taught that tapping two fingers on the table signified gratitude to the pourer.

Dessert typically consists of sliced fruit and sweetened soup with options such as chestnut, almond, and red bean, or a dumpling stuffed with lotus or red bean paste. Chocolate or anything buttery, rich, and sugary is noticeably absent from the Chinese meal, though at other Hong Kong meals I've eaten lightly-sweetened steamed cake. Most Chinese kitchens lack ovens, thus restaurants prepare desserts in a wok or steamer.

As one author commented, "There is a reason Chinese cuisine has a worldwide reputation for wontons and not for pastries."[4]

As the grazing slows down and serving platters grow empty, we combine the remaining morsels on other serving dishes. We urge one other to eat the last shrimp ball or spoonful of rice until the food is finally gone or packaged into carryout containers. The two-hour affair winds down with everyone exclaiming, "*ho bow* (I'm full)" to one another. As in most other countries, the bill is haggled over with everyone offering to pay and only one person actually forking over the cash.

I thank my generous hosts profusely, then journey home to my flat, where I eat a satisfying bite of chocolate. A perfect end to a perfect meal.

This example of a traditional local meal points to the concept of how time is viewed and practiced in Hong Kong—and how it's seemingly a paradox. "I'm too busy," is a refrain that echoes daily from the lips of city dwellers. Traffic moves at top speed. Pedestrians walk against the crosswalk lights. People run up and down escalators, which themselves move alarmingly fast. Public announcements urge travelers to refrain from pushing their way into the train and prompt citizens to be mindful of the very young and elderly. Fast movement. Pushing and shoving. Heavy traffic. Crammed schedules. Stress. This is Hong Kong.

Conversely, in this very same culture, a meal with family or friends can stretch into hours of relaxed dining, as illustrated above. An invitation to dinner often implies a multiple course spread of food complete with lively conversation and lengthy chats.

---

[4] Lee, Jennifer 8., *The Fortune Cookie Chronicles: Adventures in the World of Chinese Food* (New York: Twelve, 2008), 40.

Many restaurants practice "double booking," meaning a patron may reserve a table for two hours but must relinquish it—or, as they phrase it, "surrender it"—at a certain time for the next party. Thus demonstrating both the busyness (many people need to eat) and the leisureliness (two hours for one meal).

Hong Kong is an inconsistent city at times. But, thankfully, delicious.

CHAPTER 7

ICE AND FIDO

One adjustment I had to make early in my time in Hong Kong was getting through a restaurant meal with only small cups of tea, or learning to ration my drink because there would be no free refills.

At a traditional Hong Kong dim sum lunch, waiters serve hot tea in wee cups and saucers, which diners sip delicately and slowly. Delicious jasmine tea, boiling hot. Yet the second it reaches a less-than-scalding temperature, I throw it back like a shot glass and reach across the lazy Susan for another round. Gracious hosts around me continually refill my cup, and I bite my tongue to keep from saying, "Honey, just plant that teapot right here in front of me, thanks!"

A set meal—similar to a meal combo in the United States—usually includes a drink. But in this context, a drink means one cup of beverage sans refills, which is served after the meal. The small or medium-sized glass contains little or no ice and can be consumed in four gulps. Yet I will ration it throughout the meal. That is, once I've convinced the waiter I really do in fact desire my beverage *with* the food. Supplementary sips from my own water bottle are necessary to complete the meal.

Once settled into Hong Kong life, I joined community choir rehearsals where fellow singers surreptitiously pulled out tiny vessels for wetting their throats—cute little pink or yellow bottles no larger than a saltshaker, a suitable size for stowing in carry-on airline luggage. Local bottling companies actually sell water in diminutive bottles that hold 280 ml (9.4 fluid ounces), or about five gulps. I, on the other hand, dragged out my blue 32 oz. Nalgene and tried not to dribble water down my chin as I chugged half the bottle. And I was still thirsty.

A local woman once entered my office and exclaimed dramatically upon seeing my large—and empty—24 oz. water tumbler, "Wah! So big!"

I didn't know what to say. Should I have told her about American gas stations with their Big Gulps? Or fast-food restaurant Sonic's huge cups of delicious iced beverages? The sixteen various-sized water bottles I own? I'm not exaggerating. I just walked into my kitchen and counted them. And I got a refill of water while I was in there.

***

One Saturday afternoon as I was doing household chores in my flat, I noticed a strong stench of smoke. After ruling out the possibility of my building being on fire, I concluded that one of my neighbors had been engaging in some ritual or religious practice involving incense.

The following day, I asked a friend about this and learned that it was the Ghost Festival, or Hungry Ghost Festival. This occasion, which falls on the fourteenth night of the seventh lunar month—usually late August or early September—is observed in many different Asian countries. Some believe that on this day and throughout

Ghost Month various spirits of deceased ancestors emerge from the lower world to visit the living.

Rituals for this time include the burning of paper representations of important possessions in order to appease the dead. People burn sheets of paper, known as joss paper or, informally, "ghost money" to provide for the deceased in the afterlife. Additionally, one can purchase paper models of cars, houses, boats, clothes, cell phones, etc. to burn—again, to ensure the happiness of the departed.

I eventually learned that "hell bank notes" are another way people try to guarantee their deceased loved ones have wealth in the afterlife. Some burn these printed bills so family members can spend them in hell. The twenty-first century version resembles a credit card and is stamped with the word VISA. Apparently, credit card debt is not a significant concern in hell.

People perform these ritualistic endeavors at temples, in homes or businesses, or outside on the street. The smoldering embers are encased in a red metal pot, almost like a miniature barbecue grill, and sometimes stored in the stairwells of residential buildings. This is what I smelled that Saturday afternoon in my flat.

Throughout the following months, I began noticing an occasional mound of ashes or blackened incense sticks and fruit, typically oranges, on the sidewalk in my neighborhood. These were evidence of people following such religious practices, not only for the Hungry Ghost Festival but for other important days as well. Sweeping up the offering remains is said to bring misfortune. At some point, someone must clean it up, though, or the pavements and streets would fill up with heaps of soot and rotting produce. But I have no idea who does this.

***

Despite living in a city of seven million, I inevitably began running into the same people in my neighborhood on a regular basis. Most spoke no English, and I lacked the guts to attempt my limited Cantonese, so we rarely conversed. I didn't know their names, but they were familiar faces and a comfortable part of my routine.

When I exited my apartment complex, I frequently encountered a guard from the building across the street. Tall and lanky with thick dark hair and glasses, he ambled along the sidewalk, always wearing his uniform of navy-blue pants and a white collared shirt. He would nod, glance at me with his large eyes, and we would sometimes acknowledge one another with basic greetings.

If it was a weekday morning, I would likely see the street-sweeper. Her metal cart sat nearby, decked out with a round plastic trash bin and an assortment of rags, gloves, and cleaning implements. She swept the sidewalks and streets with her bamboo broom and tin-can dustbin. She wore the standard uniform for such employees: loose blue pants, long-sleeved shirt, and a straw hat. A piece of recycled umbrella fabric that was connected to the hat hung about her neck and protected her from the elements. When the weather was mild, her short gray hair peeked out from under her hat, and her toothy smile always revealed a full set of pearly whites.

"Leng noi," she would say to me after I said good morning in Cantonese. "Pretty girl."

Nothing to get an ego about. It's a common endearing greeting for little girls and youngish women.

On some mornings or mid-afternoons, the "skeleton man," as I thought of him, ran up my street. Reedy-thin, angular, double-jointed, and tall, this man always sprinted. Always. I never observed him walking. His bony frame jutted out of his dress shirt, one hand securing his flapping necktie, the other free to aid him as he dashed up the steep sidewalk with long strides. It was as though he was habitually late, yet he never carried any briefcase or bag. Never wore exercise attire. Where was he going? Did he run for the love of running? I never knew.

From time to time on weekdays, I'd see an ancient woman whose primary job, it seemed, was gathering cardboard and recyclables and hauling them to a nearby collection point. She was likely one of the thousands of Hong Kongers who survived on a meager income from such recycling. Of indeterminate age, her deeply wrinkled face, gnarled hands, and stringy muscles suggested a life of physically taxing labor in the sun.

Nonetheless, she would peer out at me from underneath her floppy cloth hat and display a huge toothless grin. Her eyes crinkled at the corners. She seemed happy to see me. A pang of guilt often washed over me as she passed by, her body at a forty-five-degree angle while pushing her rubbish-laden metal cart up the hill.

I should help her, I always thought to myself. Shamefully, I never offered.

There was a ten-minute time frame early on Sunday mornings in which I encountered the same elderly gentleman. His belly drooped over gray trousers, and thick silver hair hung down around his ears. His gait slow and labored, he stooped over as he walked, looking at the ground, hands clasped behind his back. A cigarette dangled from his lips, perhaps lodged in the wide gap between upper teeth. A small messenger bag was slung over one shoulder.

I didn't know where he was going, but our paths inevitably crossed, though we were moving in opposite directions. I would greet him. He would nod and smile pleasantly with a knowing look.

Maybe we hadn't seen one another in a few weeks, but today our paths had crossed again. We were both right on schedule.

On other mornings as I headed to work, a different middle-aged man passed me on my usual route. Slightly balding, clad in a light-brown jacket and green trousers, he never looked up from the sidewalk. He always clutched a small tin lunchbox in his left hand, carefully holding it parallel to the ground, while keeping his right hand in his coat pocket. The oddest aspect was the way he walked, zigzagging in diagonal lines from one edge of the sidewalk to the other. At the moment our paths were about to cross, I often froze, wondering which way I should step to avoid his next oblique turn. Although his eyes remained focused on the pavement, he never collided with anyone or anything.

A tall, big-boned older Chinese woman lived in my building with her large golden retriever. I often bumped into her and her canine companion as they were departing for, or returning from, doggie duty. She always greeted me warmly, but my unease around dogs caused me to squeeze into one corner of the elevator when we rode together. Pulling the leash closer, she spoke softly to her pet—in English. Did she always speak English to Fido? Or only when I was around?

If I was coming home late—say, between 10:30 or 11:00 p.m.—I sometimes encountered an elderly neighbor shuffling home. He looked like he should have retired decades ago, so I wasn't sure where he went every day. But he always wore sagging khaki pants, a tweed sports coat, and an aging necktie. Around 11:30 p.m., I usually smelled his cigarette smoke seeping into my flat as I settled into my bedtime preparations.

I relished routine encounters with these familiar faces and thought of them fondly. Perhaps they viewed me in a similar manner. Upon arriving home in the evening, they'd find amusement in remembering that odd American woman, a bit overeager in her greetings, who had become an entertaining fixture in their own daily schedule.

CHAPTER 8

NAMES AND MAIDS

Another aspect of Hong Kong life I found fascinating was the choice of names. As I met new people and explored various parts of the city, I encountered such creative names that I started a running list.

Names are an integral part of identity, particularly to Asians, I learned. Americans think much about the *sound* of a name or its distinctiveness, whereas to Chinese the *meaning* of a name is of greater significance. Due to the richness and uniqueness of the language, Chinese characters "paint ideas and hint at thoughts."[5] Layers of culture and meaning are implicit in a single character, thus giving depth to one's name. Attempts to replicate this language feature in English prove less successful.

A typical Hong Konger will be given a Chinese name at birth and perhaps an English name too, officially or unofficially. Quite often, though, young Hong Kongers choose their own English name. Some select a *word* rather than a *name*, displaying a spirit of

[5] Yen Mah, Adeline, *Watching the Tree* (New York: Broadway Books, 2001), 184.

individuality and imagination. Here is my list, which has continued to grow over the years.

> Able. Alien. Allegra. Almond. Apple. Bacon. Ballet. BBB. Bear. Believe. Birdie. Bobo. Bow. Bubble. Buggle. Bunny. Cable. Cake. Car. Cat. Catwina. Chloroform. Cigar. Circle. Coco. Coke. Colour. Cream. Cutina. Diamond. Dodo. Donkey. Dove. Eagle. Easy. Egg. Ego. Else. Fancy. Feecee. Fiddle. Fish. Frankly. Freedom. Freely. Fun. Future. Garfield. Gentle. Giraffe. Glacier. Godiva. Good News. Google. Green (ironically she was a trainee at a coffee shop). Happy. Hill. Horlick. Ice. Icy. Ikky. Infant. Inny. Ivory. Jackal. Jammy. Jelly. Keying. King. Lancelot. Lavender. Legward. Malaria. Milan (he worked at *Ristorante Italiano*). Milk. Molecule. Money. Monster. Moon. Mouse. Nana. Nectar. Nestle. Not. Ocean. Olive. Omegasun. Orange. Oxygen. Pansy. Paper. Peace. Persona. Piano. Pinky. Pony. Pooh. Promise. Protein. Psyche. Purple. Queenie. Quick. Rain. Rainbow. Red. Ribbon. Rice. Ringo. Rover. Royal. Seeing. Shadow. Silence. Silky. Sincere. Sixtus. Slash. Smiley. Snow. Soda. Someone. Square. Star. Starry. Steps. Sugar. Symphony. T Dollar Kong. Tangy Tang. Tinki. Tree. Triangle. Trinity. Twiggy. Unicorn. Unique. Veggie. Vitamin. Water. Wenchy. Wicky. Wilkie. Winki. Yoyo and Zealous.

***

One group I enjoyed getting to know upon arrival in Hong Kong was the Filipino community. Mostly consisting of migrant women, these individuals warmly welcomed me and took time to share with me more about Hong Kong and the Philippines. The majority of them work as a domestic helper in the home of a Hong Kong family. Due to rampant corruption, poverty, and lack of opportunities in the Philippines, these women can earn a better salary working as a maid in Hong Kong than working in other industries in the Philippines. Filipino culture places high value on family relationships, even extending beyond the immediate family, so salaries received in Hong Kong go toward supporting children, spouses, siblings, parents, and grandparents in their home country.

Hong Kong relies heavily on the domestic helper labor force, which consists of about 360,000 people, most from Southeast Asia. According to one report, domestic workers from abroad contributed an estimated US$12.6 billion to Hong Kong's economy in 2018, or 36 percent of the local GDP. Almost seventy percent of these workers are from the Philippines.[6]

These women—all of whom have a high school degree and many of whom have also earned a university degree—cook, clean, do laundry, shop for groceries, care for children and elderly, and run errands for their employer. Hiring a live-in domestic worker is significantly cheaper than childcare, and this practice allows Hong Kong women to join the workforce, creating millions of two-income families. Without this imported staff, the city would cease to function effectively.

As I got to know these hard-working women, I was surprised to learn of the Hong Kong law that requires domestic helpers to live in the homes of their employers. Residing in other accommodations is illegal. Many Hong Kong flats have a bedroom for the maid attached to the kitchen. This is typically so small that a twin mattress barely fits, extending wall-to-wall. Other helpers share a room with the children they take care of. In some scurrilous sit-

[6] Jason Hung, "Hong Kong Hurts Itself By Financially Excluding Foreign Domestic Workers," *The Diplomat*, February 7, 2020, https://thediplomat.com/2020/02/hong-kong-hurts-itself-by-financially-excluding-foreign-domestic-workers/.

uations, the maid is required to sleep in the living room, kitchen, restroom, or on the floor.

Furthermore, these women are not allowed to find additional sources of income in the city. Their visas limit them to employment with the family for whom they work. If and when their contract ends, they must exit Hong Kong within two weeks. Regardless of the number of years they live and work in the city, Filipino domestic helpers will never receive permanent residency even though immigrants from most other countries can gain such status.

Through numerous conversations with these women, I heard about the agencies that recruit Filipinos, some of which are corrupt and whose dubious practices bring about debt, abuse, and exploitation. Domestic helpers are entitled to one day off per week, usually Saturday or Sunday, but there is no limit to the number of hours their employers can require them to work on the other six days. Because they live in their employer's home, they often toil from early morning to very late at night.

Sadly, within a short time of living in Hong Kong, I began to see the pervasive discrimination against Filipinos and other domestic helpers. I observed people treating these humble women with contempt, shouting at them, or ignoring them. Others view maids with suspicion or outright disdain, perhaps because of their poor background, the general reputation of their country, or their menial position in the local workforce. This unfair and prejudicial treatment affects domestic workers of all backgrounds and ethnicities in Hong Kong.

Yet I also noticed that despite facing systemic exploitation and exhausting labor, Filipinos were some of the most cheerful, friendly people I encountered. Never had I heard such raucous laughter and joyful frivolity than when I was gathered with a group of Filipino women in our church basement. The smallest mishap, the silliest joke, or the most amusing communication blunder elicited pure hilarity—not at the expense of another, but in a spirit of camaraderie.

This was all the more striking to me when I took into account their personal lives. Many of these women have a husband and children in the Philippines whom they see once a year at most. Others remain unmarried but feel pressure from extended family to find a spouse and bear children. They face tough decisions. Should I return to the Philippines where I can be with my family, yet earn little income? Or should I stay in Hong Kong to earn more and provide a better life for my children, yet live apart from them?

The unfortunate irony is that Filipino maids often spend years with a particular Hong Kong family, raising a child or two, while their husbands, mothers, or sisters rear their own children in the Philippines. These women speak of their charges as being like a son or daughter to them. After all, they spend six days a week together. And Hong Kong children frequently spend more time with the domestic helper than with their own parents. When the helper resigns or leaves, a forced separation occurs that affects every member of this complicated situation.

I once attended a conference in which the speaker addressed issues of motherhood and marriage. During the ensuing Q&A session, a brave Filipino woman stood up and tearfully asked, "What should we say to other people when they criticize us for choosing to live and work so far away from our children? We're just trying to do what's best for them, which means getting a job in Hong Kong that pays enough to support our family."

Their struggle is evident. They tell their children in the Philippines, "Go to school and work hard so you can have a better life than I have. So you don't have to work as a maid like me."

CHAPTER 9

SNAKES AND MOONCAKES

"Have you eaten yet?" is the most common phrase Hong Kongers use when greeting someone. It's their equivalent of "How are you?"

One of the first things I learned upon moving to Hong Kong was the importance of food and gatherings around meals, so it makes sense to incorporate this into polite conversation. Numerous Hong Kongers also shared with me this Chinese witticism:

"If Adam and Eve had been Chinese, they wouldn't have eaten the forbidden fruit. They would have eaten the snake."

An appropriate and amusing introduction to culinary practices in this city. Prior to moving to Hong Kong, I speculated I might lose weight there since I would be walking more and not relying on a car to get around. This notion was quickly dispelled when I saw the amazing variety of cuisines available and began to experience the gracious hospitality of Hong Kongers who wanted to share their dietary heritage with me.

A very local style of dining I enjoyed in my first few weeks in Hong Kong is the *dai pai dong*. This dwindling age-old tradition involves eating outside at an open-air establishment. Each dai pai dong consists of a tiny, dilapidated kitchen located on the ground floor of a building. At dusk, a flurry of waiters set up a cluster of folding tables and stools on the sidewalk while hungry customers begin streaming in from surrounding streets.

Tables are covered with disposable tablecloths. As soon as diners vacate a table, new customers sit down. Waiters quickly replace the tablecloth, then plunk down one well-worn menu along with an old canister of toothpicks, a partially-used roll of toilet paper, a plastic pitcher of hot tea, and enough bowls, cups, and chopsticks for each person.

On my first such outing, several friends and I joined together to order dinner. The food arrived quickly, steaming hot and deliciously aromatic. In this casual atmosphere, formalities such as serving chopsticks, the chopstick rest, and a lazy Susan were absent. Everyone dug in and helped themselves, holding bowls close to the mouth as food was consumed.

We enjoyed lemon-fried chicken, bak choi and choi sum vegetables cooked in garlic, fresh scallops, *congee* (rice porridge), and small fish. Individual bowls of rice were optional. I ate a tasty dish containing frog—not frog legs, but small chunks of frog meat mixed up with veggies and rice. It didn't taste like chicken, as frog is so often stereotyped, but it was good.

Due to my amateur chopstick skills, I was the only person who required a napkin. Or in this case, some of the toilet tissue placed on the table for this purpose. Scraps, including chicken bones, fish skeletons, and shellfish parts, were placed directly on the table. Upon finishing the meal, toothpicks were employed, the bill paid, dishes removed, and the disposable tablecloth gathered up and dropped into the rubbish bin.

After eating, we moved on down the street to stroll through the night markets, local shops, and other snack stands. It was a delightful way to spend a summer Hong Kong evening.

* * *

Later, I took a taxi home. Like the minibus drivers, most taxi drivers in Hong Kong have on display random knick knacks such as a mini Buddha statue, a good-luck charm hanging from the rearview mirror, an air-freshener attached to the vent, or a Hello Kitty item. But some decorate in excess, filling the dashboard so that it looks like a miniature toy museum.

On this single taxi ride, I saw these treasures. A tiny basket of artificial flowers. A colorful octopus-like creature swinging from the rearview mirror. Magnetic toy cars lining the bottom of the mirror. A bobble-head Chinese dragon. A diminutive plastic man with his legs hanging off the dashboard. The tiny man held a fishing rod that dangled over the ledge, complete with tiny fish attached. As if to represent a sea for this fisherman, several plastic fish were affixed to the outside of the glove compartment.

I suppose if I drove a vehicle identical to thousands of others, I might also make an effort to creatively distinguish my taxi. Or fill it with toys to help pass the time.

* * *

Early in the fall, I experienced one of my first local holidays, the Mid-Autumn Festival. This is observed on the fifteenth day of the eighth month of the lunar calendar, usually in September or early October in the Gregorian calendar. In Chinese culture, a round shape symbolizes unity, and the full moon is a reminder of home, family, and harmony. The importance of this celestial body in Asian tradition is evidenced in a fragment of an ancient Chinese poem that reads, "May we live long and share the beauty of the moon together, even if we are hundreds of miles apart."[7]

Also called the Moon Festival, this holiday is a time of family gatherings, festive dinners, lantern displays, and mooncakes. Historically, celebrants constructed lanterns out of paper or rattan and utilized real candles. Unsurprisingly—and gratefully—I noted that most lanterns nowadays were the safer battery-operated kind fashioned of plastic, many in the shape of cartoon characters or other pop culture icons.

Parks and public areas were decorated with elaborate exhibits. Families with children strolled around with their individual lanterns, snapping photos of giant, brightly-lit figures or checking out carnival-like exhibitions. Though I'd heard there would be dragon dance performances on this holiday, I never did see one.

Of that first Mid-Autumn Festival, my most vivid memory is the mooncake. I liken this pastry to holiday fruitcakes in the United States or Europe. You either love them or hate them, and they are frequently given, re-gifted, or re-re-gifted to friends and colleagues. The traditional Cantonese-style mooncake is roughly the size of a hockey puck, round with scalloped edges, and imprinted with intricate designs of flowers or Chinese calligraphy. A true work of art. The outer dough is thin, and the inside is chewy and thick, consisting of cooked egg yolk—not surprisingly, a symbol of the moon—and lotus paste.

In recent years, companies have started creating a variety of different flavors, styles, and types of mooncakes. My favorite is a

[7] "Celebrate in Hong Kong with these time-honoured festivities," Hong Kong Tourism Board, accessed November 2, 2017, http://www.discoverhongkong.com/eng/see-do/events-festivals/chinese-festivals/mid-autumn-festival.jsp.

Häagen-Dazs ice cream version. The box in which mooncakes are packaged is often ornate, worthy of keeping long after celebrants devour the treat. But the devouring must be done at a slow pace. A mooncake is dense, heavy, and rich, best cut in small wedges, shared among friends, and consumed with a cup of strong Chinese tea.

Or passed along unopened to another friend who would enjoy it more.

CHAPTER 10

TRASH AND RAGPICKERS

Early in my time in Hong Kong, I took note of my trash in comparison to that of my neighbors. The floor of the building in which I lived contained four flats. These residents and I shared one large garbage can located in the stairwell. A building caretaker came to empty this barrel each morning—weekends and holidays included.

I had a medium-sized trashcan in my kitchen, which I emptied once or twice a week. When I gathered up my garbage and hauled it to the stairwell bin, I saw tiny plastic sacks filled with my neighbors' refuse. They might have discarded a few vegetable scraps, a handful of tissue, and perhaps a few other items—all in a thin produce sack. Meanwhile, my enormous trash bag was stuffed with granola bar wrappings, cracker packages, soiled paper towels, juice and milk cartons, chip bags, and more.

This rubbish assessment was indicative of where we shopped and the products we purchased. Which were in turn evidence of our cultural backgrounds—and my unhealthy eating habits. My neighbors likely bought produce, meat, and dairy at a local market where food was not pre-packaged. I picked up groceries at a Western-style supermarket where much of the food came enveloped in Styrofoam, plastic, or paper. Many Hong Kongers shop frequently, even daily, in order to have fresh food. I shopped once a week and stocked up on canned items and dry goods.

This recurring trip to the stairwell rubbish bin made me keenly aware of how wasteful I was. Why couldn't I re-use zipper-sealed bags? A rag or sponge worked in most cases as well as a paper towel. Could I not be more intentional about carrying my own water bottle rather than buying a beverage in a can or plastic bottle? Why toss out a paper shopping bag when it could be used later for disposing trash?

On most mornings as I headed out for work, I encountered the building caretaker who was responsible for emptying the bins. She spoke no English, and I never had a successful conversation with her in Cantonese. But she had a way of looking me up and down and talking *at* me every time we encountered one another. I would smile and greet her, but I sensed her disapproval. She could have been saying something benign such as, "Lovely day, isn't it?" or "I like your blouse." But over the years, I began to imagine her thinking and even saying aloud, "That dim-witted foreigner throws away so much rubbish! From one person, huge bags of trash!"

On some occasions when I saw this woman, I found her pointing at me and speaking to another tenant or building employee in Cantonese. Presumably, I was the topic of discussion, a bit like talking about me behind my back *and* right to my face. I also witnessed her habit of sifting through the building garbage, perhaps to separate out recyclables or salvage useable items.

I found it profoundly humbling to know someone was looking through the worst of what I had and was. So I strove to become more mindful of what I bought, how I used or re-used it, and how

I disposed of it. I'd like to say I did this only out of concern for the environment as a caring citizen of God's creation. In truth, it was also a matter of pride and an odd desire for approval from the custodian of my building.

***

Resourcefulness and ingenuity are characteristics evident in many Hong Kong residents regardless of economic status. I am continually impressed by their use of discarded objects to meet a need and their think-outside-the-box manner of addressing everyday problems.

Some examples: Envelopes from the mail are opened, emptied, marked out, refilled, and re-mailed. A bicycle commuter, concerned that the cuffs of his pant legs may get caught in the wheels, pins up his trousers with clothespins. Another cyclist fashions wheel fenders out of sections of a disposable water bottle. In the event of a heavy downpour, a large upside-down garbage bag may function as a raincoat or be attached to a hat brim as a makeshift umbrella.

This making use of the resources at hand pervades Hong Kong society. Function and practicality frequently trump aesthetic appearance. Entire sections of this city look jimmy-rigged and at risk of falling apart in a strong wind. Ancient air conditioning units are fastened high onto the side of a building using a rusted metal brace, a tangled mess of wires hanging below. Older structures have corrugated-sheet-metal awnings or homemade television antennas poking out. Vendor booths fill street markets, each constructed of aluminum poles covered with scraps of tarp and plastic sheeting.

In addition to resourcefulness, taking care of the environment is also a characteristic of many Hong Kongers, especially important in a city containing seven million people squeezed onto a relatively small plot of land. Hong Kong instituted a plastic bag fee in mid-2009 to encourage customers to bring their own reusable shopping bags. This followed a common public service announcement: "BYOB (bring your own bag)." Some fast food restaurants and universities are "no straw zones." Napkins aren't always offered at restaurants, though an onionskin-like tissue may be available.

I've attended potluck meals in which individuals brought their own metal utensils rather than eating on paper plates with plastic cutlery. Disposable chopsticks—available at every food stall, convenience store, and fast-food restaurant—are often shunned. Many schools ask students to bring their own fork, spoon, and chopsticks even when purchasing a school lunch. In shopping malls, janitors use large tongs to remove pieces of trash from smaller bins, thus saving the garbage can liner.

Additionally, hundreds of ragpickers—referred to locally as "cardboard grannies"—work all over the city gathering cardboard boxes and other bits and bobs. These are deposited at recycling collection points as a source of income. Because of this scavenging industry, residents can leave a sack of discarded clothing or other unwanted items on the curb, and it is certain to be picked up and used or resold by someone.

Ironically, a local English newspaper once published an interview with an environmental activist who argued that Hong Kong had too many rubbish bins, which he claimed contributed to increased generation of waste. Apparently, the abundance of trash receptacles in the city—42,000 according to this 2014 article—encouraged a "culture of convenience."[8]

[8] Ernest Kao, "Huge number of rubbish bins in Hong Kong is contributing to waste crisis, says activist," *South China Morning Post*, December 29, 2014, https://www.scmp.com/news/hong-kong/article/1670243/huge-number-rubbish-bins-hong-kong-contributing-waste-crisis-says.

At the other end of the spectrum, wastefulness and consumerism exist as a reality in Hong Kong. Many people seem unaware of the need to recycle, instead dropping aluminum soda cans in a trash receptacle sitting next to a recycling bin. For city dwellers who don't own a car, it's much more difficult to donate or upcycle furniture and other bulky items. Very few secondhand shops exist in Hong Kong, although classified ad apps spring up often.

In terms of extravagance, many top names in the luxury fashion industries can be found in this shopping Mecca of the East, including Dior, Gucci, Chanel, and Louis Vuitton. The skyscrapers around the harbor offer a glimpse of the technology and financial sectors: AIG, Hitachi, Philips, Samsung, Olympus, Toshiba, Epson, Sharp, and Sanyo, to name a few. Posh flats, top-of-the-line automobiles, trendy suits, the latest technological gadgets, and high-priced dining and entertainment seem to define life for much of the populace.

These two divergent characteristics of Hong Kong—resourcefulness and extravagance—also highlight the vast gap between the rich and the poor. In the decade of the 2010s, the cost of residential property rose by over two hundred percent.[9] Hong Kong usually tops the global list of the most unaffordable places to live due to astronomical rent and property prices. With housing costs so high, a number of destitute Hong Kongers live in "caged homes" or "coffin homes"—minuscule personal spaces consisting only of a small pallet surrounded by wire mesh. Others live in subdivided flats, which offer a few dozen square feet within a partitioned apartment.

[9] Thomas Peter, "Why Hong Kong's angry and disillusioned youth are making their voices heard," *Post Magazine*, July 22, 2019, https://www.scmp.com/magazines/post-magazine/long-reads/article/3019591/why-hong-kongs-angry-and-disillusioned-youth-are.

Both options are only one tiny step above homelessness. Residents of these unsafe, abhorrent conditions "include elderly, low-skilled workers, and others who have fallen through society's cracks."[10] With insufficient welfare and retirement provisions, the future is bleak for many indigent locals.

Hong Kong is an incongruous city.

[10] Rachel Yeo and Sue Ng, "Beyond laser pointers and tear gas: the history of Sham Shui Po, Hong Kong's poorest district," *South China Morning Post*, August 24, 2019, https://www.scmp.com/news/hong-kong/politics/article/3023974/beyond-laser-pointers-and-tear-gas-history-sham-shui-po.

CHAPTER 11

SHRIMP AND NAPS

Large saltwater tanks in which fish floated lethargically. Outdoor canopied dining spaces along a seaside boardwalk crammed with tables surrounded by plastic stools and chairs. The strong, briny scent of the ocean. Residents strolling along the waterfront. These were my first impressions of Sai Kung, a seaside district in the New Territories.

Some new friends had invited me to dinner. They picked me up in their car to drive out to this less-populated corner of Hong Kong. Leaving the vehicle in a carpark, we walked down a few darkened streets to the wharf where all the noted seafood places were situated. Each restaurant had an area where shallow open-top tanks of water were stacked together on tiers, packed with an assortment of sea creatures. There were fish of all kinds, plus shrimp, lobster, crab, oysters, clams, scallops, squid, calamari, and other types of unrecognizable crustaceans.

Workers clad in galoshes moved around the tanks, walking on thin boards between the reservoirs. They were busy pulling out sea creatures and draining and refilling tanks. It was a malodorous, wet place, and I got splashed more than once as I examined the dinner options.

Arriving at our chosen restaurant, we settled at a round table surrounded by aging deck chairs. My friends studied the menu and chose a set meal that contained five courses of seafood plus a vegetable and a noodle dish. We began with shrimp, lightly boiled and deliciously fresh. As is customary in Hong Kong, we were served the whole shrimp, a situation that required me to labor for the tiny morsels of goodness. Not being skilled at this endeavor, it took me a long time to get to the meat. Plus, each shrimp contained a brown substance that inevitably exploded all over me when I tried to pop the head off.

After five or six prawns, I started to get the hang of the process and decided the effort was worth it. This was some of the most delicious fresh shrimp I had ever tasted. One of my dinner companions commented that many people eat the heads of shrimp, but he preferred not to because the head contained too much cholesterol. I nodded in agreement. Yes, I also had no desire to eat the head. I neglected to mention that my motive was not necessarily the result of concern for health.

We left the less favorable seafood parts on our plates. The waiters soon removed our dishes and brought clean ones, a practice repeated after each course. We were also given bowls of warm water containing lemon slices for cleansing our fishy hands. While there's something to be said for de-veined and shelled shrimp eaten with a fork, as I grew up eating, nothing beats the freshness of Hong Kong seafood—cholesterol-laden heads and all.

Our seafood feast continued with lobster, some type of shellfish, and a kind of white flatfish so tender it melted in my mouth. We also partook of a larger version of prawn with a purple tint on the outside, flavored with spices and salt. These were so large it seemed oxymoronic to call them "shrimp." Each one provided several bites of savory meat.

I asked the name of this delicious sea creature. My friends pronounced the name in Cantonese, then glanced at each other before remarking that it was hard to translate. Anyway, they added, the name didn't really convey what it was. Upon seeing my confused look, they stumbled around to describe the phrase used for the species of prawn.

"It's something like 'unable to hold urine,'" one friend said.

"Incontinence," added the other.

Neither knew how this food came to have such an incongruous name, and I dared not ask further questions. Later, I researched this and discussed it with other Hong Kongers. Apparently, the creature is a type of mantis shrimp. But its Cantonese name translates to "urine shrimp" due to its propensity to squirt a stream of water when picked up. An unpleasant topic of conversation for the dinner table, indeed.

Like all Chinese dinners, the food came little by little rather than all at once. The tables were so close to one another that strangers continually bumped into me. The heightened crowd noise made personal conversation frustrating. Also, it took several lemon slices and a long session of handwashing to remove the fishy smell from my hands when I arrived home.

Nevertheless, with a breeze from the ocean drifting over us, the fragrance of steaming vegetables and garlic in the air, and the fresh seafood pleasing my palate, the evening was lovely. This laid-back dinner in Sai Kung was a welcome break from the hectic feeling of ordinary Hong Kong life.

***

Previously, I'd considered Americans to be workaholics. We have little annual vacation time. We take pride in saying, "I'm too busy." We have a tendency to define ourselves by our careers. Contrast this with the long summer holidays taken in some European nations, the weekday siesta still observed in many Latin American communities, and the more laidback lifestyle found in Southeast Asia, Africa, and numerous island nations.

When I moved to Hong Kong though, I was stunned by the pace of life and work there. The diligence and industriousness of Hong Kongers was unparalleled. Long working hours, six-or seven-day workweeks, late-night international conference calls, frequent business trips, and short lunch breaks characterize a typical Hong Konger's life. This is a busy city. Even children are pressured into rigorous schedules, including lengthy school hours, extra tutoring and lessons after school, weekend tutorials and music trainings, hours and hours of homework, test reviews, and projects. There's a reason some of the most brilliant and successful people in the world are Asian.

That said, I soon noticed this stress permeates every aspect of life in Hong Kong.

People rush from one destination to another, creating an atmosphere of urgency and chaos. Even the escalators and elevators run at an alarmingly high speed. Friendships are difficult to maintain since long working hours hinder the development of relationships. Families are in crisis because parents work late and all members have less quality time together.

The Hong Kong lifestyle pace is pressed upon children from infancy onward. Many parents feel they must get their toddlers into the best preschools and kindergartens so they can qualify for entrance into the top grade schools. A child is expected to learn other skills from early childhood, such as violin, Mandarin, badminton, or ballet, so their university résumé will have a firm foundation. This mindset begins from birth. Scheduled C-sections are common.

* * *

The result of this hectic lifestyle was evident one warm afternoon as I was walking through a local park. An elderly gentleman sat on a low stool, his head bobbing in a sleepy daze. He reminded me of a drowsy toddler falling asleep in a highchair over a plate of spaghetti, desperately trying to stay awake but losing the fight. As I watched, the man began to fall—literally in slow motion—off the short stool. His body gradually sank to the ground until he ended up in a squat. Startled, he awoke and managed to use his hands to keep his balance.

I had already begun to hurry toward the elderly gentleman when he seemed to stabilize on his knees and start to rise. Either too sleepy or too frail, he sank and teetered again, unable to straighten his legs and stand up from this awkward squatting position. He wasn't in danger of hurting himself, but he was at risk of landing on his tail on the dirty ground. Reaching him, I grabbed his arm to help him up. At the same time, two other bystanders also came over to assist.

By then, the man had regained his balance and managed to reseat himself on the stool.

I asked if he was okay, but he waved me away impatiently. I'm certain he felt embarrassed, but at least he survived the sleepy scare unscathed. I chuckled through the remainder of the day as I thought of this man's languid, slow-motion slouch from the stool. Perhaps he should return to his home and make use of a comfy armchair.

Due to the bustling lifestyle, Hong Kong is a city desperately in need of rest, filled with sleep-deprived citizens. Everywhere I look, I see Hong Kongers nodding off in impromptu naps. On the bus or train, heads sinking down or jerking up in a sleepy head-bob. On park benches or picnic tables, people stretching out for a lunchtime rest or afternoon siesta. Taxi drivers display their "out of service" sign in the windshield and take a snooze while parked on the side of the road. Construction workers and street sweepers huddle in a corner or against a brick wall with newspaper draped over their faces, catching forty winks during a break.

I'm thankful that most of these heavy-eyed Hong Kongers don't drive, instead opting for public transportation. I'd rather sit next to a snoring woman on a bus than look over at a stoplight and see a dozing driver in the next vehicle.

CHAPTER 12

ROBBERS AND CHARADES

Hong Kongers may keep hectic schedules and suffer from a lack of sleep, but I found that many of them care much about fitness and exercise. From time to time, I visited the neighborhood park, which has a delightful walking track through a tree-lined garden. Sometimes I was one of the youngest people there. Retirees in Hong Kong are astonishingly diligent about engaging in physical activity. Grandmas inched down the track in their sneakers, cane in use. Grandpas meandered along the trail, hands clasped behind their backs. Older couples strolled silently together.

One such elderly man, who looked like he could be approaching the century mark, engaged in dangerous feats of gymnastics on the park's parallel bars. He always wore gray sweatpants, tattered canvas shoes, and the same orange-and-blue button-down shirt. His spindly legs and arms grasped the bars while his body balanced precariously. His feet and hands stretched as his torso raised and lowered in a push-up motion. His face was drawn taut, his cheeks so sunken most of his facial bones showed.

I couldn't figure out how the elderly man could maneuver the equipment with such ease, not to mention courage. I wouldn't dare try climbing on those bars even with rubber-soled tennis shoes. And he would do this the entire time I was walking laps around the park.

I frequently crossed paths with another elderly man in this same park, though he and I had never stopped for a conversation. I came to recognize him by his familiar blue plaid shirt and shuffled gait. One day, I ran into him on my street for the first time in several months. Surprised to see him in a different location, I greeted him. In return, he commented that he hadn't seen me exercising in the park lately. When I responded that I'd been busy, he chided me for not being more faithful.

"Keeping fit is important," he remarked, patting his belly.

There's nothing like being reprimanded about not staying in shape by a man two-and-a-half times my age who moves like a tortoise. This was not the same man, by the way, who one morning as I left my flat pointed to his stomach, then to mine, and said perhaps the only English word he knew. "Baby?"

A shot to the self-esteem indeed. It seemed clear I should follow the example of the elderly around me and redirect some of the busyness of my Hong Kong life toward exercise. But I preferred taking a nap. Or eating.

***

I discovered an Italian restaurant in Hong Kong that quickly became one of my favorites. The food was decent, but more importantly, they offered free refills on iced tea. The free refills then compelled me to visit the ladies' room, where I was amused to hear a "learn to speak conversational Italian" recording over the PA. While washing my hands, I listened to a stilted dialogue about locating a seat on the train or navigating an airport check-in counter.

No matter the topic, only two voices spoke: a teacher voice, i.e., the native Italian, and a student voice, i.e., the visiting foreigner. Every line of the scripted discussion was spoken in both Italian and English in a deliberate, pedantic tone. For example:

Foreigner: "Are there any rooms available in this hotel?"

Italian: "Yes."

Foreigner: "How much does a room cost?"

Italian: "It depends on how many people are staying."

Periodically, a pause in the short exchange occurred, and a new topic arose. One day, I heard such a bizarre conversation that I ran back to my table and scribbled it down, startling the friend with whom I was eating.

Foreigner: "What should I do if I meet a robber?"

Italian: "Do not resist him."

Foreigner: "Why?"

Italian: "He may have a knife or a gun."

Foreigner: "Will he try to hurt me?"

Italian: "Yes."

Foreigner: "What should I do?"

Italian: "You should give him what he wants."

Foreigner: "What if I do not have what he wants?"

Italian: "You should always carry money for a robber."

Always carry extra cash to give to a thief. Wisdom often comes from the unlikeliest of sources. And in the unlikeliest of places.

***

Despite the prevalence of English, it's still common to encounter local Hong Kongers who prefer Cantonese or have limited English skills, especially when I'm traveling in the New Territories. Due to my own ignorance and inability to master Cantonese, my communication is often reduced to monosyllables, incomplete sentences, and a variety of charade-type actions.

On one occasion early in my time in Hong Kong, I went to a department store in search of bed sheets, which ended up requiring me to use charades. All packages of bedding contained a bottom sheet and several pillowcases. In my quest for a top sheet, I made repeated attempts of acting like I was crawling into bed and pulling a sheet over me. When I realized I was drawing the attention of other customers as well as completely baffling the salesclerks, I gave up. Later, I learned that Hong Kongers followed the British custom of using duvet covers, so a top sheet wasn't customary. Thereafter, I purchased my linens in the United States.

Sound effects can also be useful in conversation. I'm not afraid to swallow my pride to help out strangers with this peculiar communication skill. While I was shopping at a hobby store, a young Middle Eastern man came to the checkout counter where I was paying for my items. He asked if the clerk had an air horn in stock, describing it in such a way that I understood his inquiry. The salesclerk, in contrast, appeared clueless.

I felt sorry for the young man, having experienced this kind of situation numerous times myself. So I turned to the salesperson and vocalized the blaring sound of an air horn. After a moment of shocked silence, a light of recognition registered on the clerk's face, and he directed the customer to another section of the store.

I felt I deserved a commendation of gratitude from the young man. Maybe even a sales discount from the store employee as reward for my heroic efforts. Alas, I only received a few curious glances and raised eyebrows from them both. I quietly paid for my items and left.

In another instance, my attempt to facilitate a successful conversation ended up backfiring on me. I called the local gas company as I was experiencing problems with my hot water heater. After I verified that the customer service agent spoke "some English" (those were her words), I began an overly dramatic description of my issue.

"I am having a problem with my hot water heater," I said, using my "special English" voice. This irksome habit includes speaking slowly with pauses between every word, enunciating each part of the sentence. "When I turn on my shower, the water gets very, very cold. And then, when I do *not* touch the water handle, the water gets very, very hot. And then cold. And then hot. And then cold. *Aiyaa!* No good!"

To my chagrin, the woman responded politely, "So the temperature of your hot water heater is inconsistent?"

Indeed. Effective communication had taken place despite my ridiculous garble.

One side note. *Aiyaa*—my favorite Cantonese word—is not actually Cantonese nor a word as much as it is a verbal utterance of annoyance or exasperation. I once heard an American television sitcom character voice this expression in the midst of a monologue in Mandarin. The on-screen English subtitles translated it into the Yiddish oy vey.

One of my biggest challenges in dealing with people cross-culturally is trying to determine if our misunderstanding, issue, or miscommunication is due to personality differences or cultural discrepancies. In other words, is this person exhibiting their own disposition or conforming to their cultural upbringing or some combination of both? Determining the answer to that question affects how I would proceed in our interaction.

On the other hand, this interplay of characteristics can work in my favor too. In Hong Kong when I find myself saying or doing something peculiar, I inwardly smile, realizing onlookers will not necessarily think, "*Angie* is odd and strange," but rather, "*Americans* are odd and strange." I take comfort in the idea that my personal eccentricities can be blamed on the entire United States population. (Deepest apologies, of course, to my fellow Americans who have been judged by this particular lunatic's behavior.)

CHAPTER 13

YAMS AND DING-DINGS

When I was growing up, my favorite holiday was always Thanksgiving. During my first year in Hong Kong, I wondered how celebrating the holiday here would compare. An American friend invited me to join her family and others for a feast, which we scheduled for a Saturday in late November since Thanksgiving Day is not actually a holiday in Hong Kong.

I soon learned that Thanksgiving preparation here began weeks and even months beforehand. A turkey could be difficult to locate, not to mention outrageously expensive. Most Hong Kong flats don't have a full-sized oven, and neither did my friend's flat, so the best option was a small turkey or a pre-cooked turkey breast.

Thankfully, the Western supermarkets that catered to American and European expats stocked up on holiday products in the fall. We were able to purchase turkey gravy, cranberry sauce, packaged stuffing mixes, olives, pickles, and other side dishes. Canned yams were more difficult to track down and particularly treasured upon discovery. Hong Kong does have fresh purple sweet potatoes, which are delicious, but these are not a suitable substitute for the American canned variety when making a candied yam casserole.

Emails and text messages flew amongst those of us participating in this feast. "I found cornbread dressing! Has anyone seen canned pumpkin lately? Which store has fresh cranberries nowadays?"

Of particular value were french-fried onions for use in the green bean casserole, a classic dish in the Southern US. Any time I found a package of them in a store, I grabbed it, not knowing if we would see the product again. I've often wondered, should a fire break out in my flat and I can only grab three items before fleeing, would I have time to get to the can of french-fried onions?

***

To illustrate the challenges of our holiday treasure hunt shopping, a few years after this first Thanksgiving feast, Hong Kong experienced a scarcity of shortening. For months, we searched the land in vain for a can of Crisco. By Christmastime, it was clear a full-blown shortening shortage existed throughout the city. It became a topic of discussion with every Westerner we encountered.

"Have you seen Crisco lately? Did you look at that one store on the island? How much do you have left? Can stick butter or margarine be substituted for shortening in pumpkin pie? Could you ask your cousin to bring some when she comes through Asia next month?"

Finally, in July of the next year, lard became available again. Meanwhile, we expats had hoarded the remaining cupfuls, treating them as valuable commodities, never squandering them in subpar baking. I even briefly considered opening a black-market operation in Crisco distribution.

***

Going back to that Saturday of my first Hong Kong Thanksgiving, I awoke early, collected my gastronomic offerings, and trekked over to the flat of my friend who was hosting the event. Others were arriving with their own contributions. As we gathered, we pretended it was lunchtime on the fourth Thursday of November in Anytown, USA. The television was playing a recorded copy of the previous year's Macy's Thanksgiving Day Parade. The small countertop toaster oven was in full use. The turkey and stove-top stuffing was warmed, casseroles assembled, potatoes mashed, and relish trays set out for pre-dinner munching.

Kitchens in Hong Kong are typically quite compact, making the preparations a challenge. Nonetheless, my friend did an amazing job of readying this authentic American feast, and we all enjoyed recounting past Thanksgiving traditions and memories as our mouths watered in anticipation.

At last, we all gathered around the loaded table, offered gratitude to God, and dove in, heaping our plates with the delicacies. More people were in attendance than could fit around the dining table, so we sprawled out on furniture and chairs or on the floor. Non-American friends were in attendance, so we explained the customs associated with this holiday. Later, we challenged one another to a game of "write down all fifty states as fast as you can." I was humiliated to lose out to a Brit.

The evening came to an end with pecan and pumpkin pies, atop of which sat mounds of soft vanilla ice cream or homemade whipped topping. We bade one another farewell, then headed out to the bustling public transportation filled with people who had just experienced an ordinary day.

The next day would be yet another ordinary day. No Black Friday sales to line up for. No leftover turkey sandwiches since we'd eaten it all. No weekend football games to watch on television. Yet we'd observed this holiday with a particularly grateful spirit. After all, we might not get a taste of those rationed french-fried onions for another year.

* * *

The following November, a local Western supermarket's website boasted "Crazy Thanksgiving Day Deals." A click on the ad brought up their idea of necessary products for this holiday: beer, sparking water, Japanese rice noodles, Mr. Juicy Juice, milk powder, and dried Craisins. That was it. Needless to say, I was disappointed.

This same store occasionally held international "food festivals," in which they would import special products from a particular country for a period of time—Britain, Germany, or Japan, for example. I grew excited one day when I learned they were featuring the United States. I rushed eagerly to the aisle draped in American flags, while visions of Ranch dressing and cinnamon gum danced in my head.

My joy turned to sadness when I studied the display. There was Kool-Aid, wine-flavored ice cream, organic Sesame Street cookies for toddlers, canned sardines, Elmo-themed vegetable soup, Gummi Army Guys and Jet Fighters, an off-brand Oreo knock-off, bratwurst, and corn nuts. Really? This was the best my country could export?

Thankfully, in the many years since my first Thanksgiving there, much has changed in Hong Kong. Today American foods and Thanksgiving ingredients are more widely available. And with advances in technology, the internet, and television streaming services it's now possible to watch current football games and parades instead of taped reruns.

***

During my first fall in Hong Kong, I experienced two more forms of public transportation: the ferry and tram. Because of where I lived and worked, these rides were more of a novelty than a convenient mode of transport for me.

The green-and-white Star Ferry, a Hong Kong icon, serves as both a tourist attraction and a practical form of daily commute for many residents. Crossing Victoria Harbour, this remnant of the past provides impressive views of the waterfront and city skyline backed by majestic mountains.

Each Star Ferry contains two decks. I chose the lower deck for my first ferry crossing, marveling at the long wooden benches, which have reversible metal backs so travelers can sit facing either direction. Though a lovely breeze wafted in through the open sides, a sickening gasoline smell permeated the area around the roaring engine.

As we passengers exited after the ten-minute journey, I experienced a few moments of sea legs while wobbling across the bumpy plank toward solid ground. Perhaps the most interesting part of the journey was the conversational exchanges I heard on board as sightseers from all over the world enjoyed the ferry. On this aging, yet idyllic boat, I had the impression I was experiencing a harbor crossing seventy-five years back in time in a remote European colony on a subtropical island.

Another blast from the past is the streetcar-like tram on Hong Kong Island. A friend introduced me to the tram system. We decided to sit on the upper deck, so we climbed the narrow stairs to the top. The tramcars were not air-conditioned, but they provided charming views of street scenes from above. Open windows brought in a gentle wind—and a rain shower. Thus, I quickly discovered the perils of sitting in the upper front seat.

Referred to as "ding-dings" because of their metallic bells, this distinctive mode of transportation dates back to 1904. Trams rumble down metal tracks in the center of busy multi-lane streets, surrounded by double-decker buses, delivery trucks, private cars, and taxis. Clattering slowly through the urban landscape, the trams represent a piece of history as well as contemporary life since they are covered with brightly-colored ads and artwork. Despite technological advances in Hong Kong's other transport systems, the humble trams carry on unchanged year after year, rattling and clanging through the city against a backdrop of shiny glass commercial towers.

Early twentieth-century trams weaving among twenty-first century skyscrapers. The old and the new side by side. Classic Hong Kong.

CHAPTER 14

HARDHATS AND BEES

The profusion of noise gives evidence to the toil and industry of Hong Kongers. It is one aspect of the city I disliked on arrival and to which I've never fully adjusted. Crowded living conditions, crammed neighborhoods, countless high-rise buildings, and seven million people packed together on a few hundred square miles of terra firma don't add up to a quiet existence.

Because I live in an aging building, workers are routinely carrying out renovations in one of the flats, which results in excruciating racket all day. Sounds of banging, hammering, pounding, jackhammers, and drilling fill my home from morning to late afternoon. Depending on the proximity of the renovation, my walls may literally shake and vibrate.

When I step outside to escape the mayhem, similar construction din abounds in the streets all around my neighborhood. When I stroll down the sidewalks, I pass people talking loudly or walking their barking dogs. I've often passed two people having a conversation, each holding a handful of leashes while their respective packs of canines howl at one another.

If I board a bus, people are chatting on their mobile phones. If I hop on a train, I'm jostled on all sides by more noisy people. If I ride in a taxi, the squawking CB radio and cacophonous Canto-pop music nearly drive me crazy. It's not uncommon for a cab driver to have music playing, the CB radio turned up, and multiple ringing phones laid out on the dashboard.

Once in a fit of exasperation, I tried escaping to a local swimming pool on my day off from work. I found it equally tumultuous—packed with people, surrounded by tall buildings undergoing construction, situated near highways with honking cars, belching buses, and screeching trucks.

In the middle of the night, blessed silence may be punctuated by chirping birds. It might be 3:00 a.m. with the sun not yet risen, but the flying creatures are apparently confused by the city lights and begin their morning song. As soon as daylight does peek over the tall buildings, street sweepers start their work on the neighborhood sidewalks. I never knew a broom could be loud, but they are indeed. Stiff bamboo leaves and shoots attached to a bamboo pole make quite a disturbance on the brick-covered pavement.

I cannot get away from noise. No wonder so many Hong Kongers walk around with headphones and earbuds on.

***

Construction is the primary source of racket, an ever-present industry in a city splitting at the seams. With population growth, newly-acquired wealth pouring over the border from Mainland China, limited housing options, and aging infrastructure, building and renovation work can be seen on every block. I've studied a number of construction sites in Hong Kong, and these are some of my observations.

Bamboo scaffolding. This is a marvelous feat of engineering combined with ancient wisdom and guts that I continue to be impressed by, no matter how many times I see it. One brave soul leans out a seventeenth-floor window and affixes a metal bracket to the side of the building. With one leg on that bracket and one arm grasping the windowsill, the worker installs another bracket into place. The safety harness loosely draped across his waist may or may not be attached to something on the other end.

Next, he lays out two or three bamboo poles across the brackets. Then another guy climbs out and begins lashing more poles together with nylon strips. Eventually, several workers are hanging off various windows and brackets, fastening poles together, as those on the ground hand up more bamboo. After hours or even days, the result is a geometric network of stout wicker stretching across buildings or entire blocks, as strong as modern-day metal scaffolding.

Covered buildings. To cut down on dust and debris from construction, workers hang giant net-like tarps over buildings. Usually green or white in color, this drapery gives the appearance of a mysterious shroud or veil. I once watched several workers drop white tulle over a building in my neighborhood. As it gracefully unfurled from ten stories above, I felt as if grand wedding preparations were underway.

Primitive tools. A beat-up wheelbarrow pushed by a shirtless man. Two women shoveling heaps of broken concrete by hand. Workers carrying plastic buckets of construction materials here and there. Wicker baskets filled with cement debris. The process looks more like a do-it-yourself Saturday morning project in the backyard than the assembly of a multi-billion-dollar housing estate in a modern world city. But why change methodologies when this approach is clearly working well?

Lack of safety mechanisms. I've watched a welder who wasn't wearing safety goggles and a guy running a jackhammer while wearing canvas sneakers, sweatpants, and a T-shirt. I once saw a man operating a backhoe balanced precariously on top of a pile of rubble. He was literally digging into the very mound that supported his machinery.

On narrow, crowded sidewalks and streets where ongoing work is taking place, it's impossible for pedestrians to completely avoid construction areas. There are times when I feel I should be wearing a hardhat, simply because I'm walking so close to manual laborers and heavy machinery or underneath rickety-looking scaffolding. But I just stick in my earbuds and keep going.

***

All this regional construction creates heavy pollution, and it wasn't long after moving to Hong Kong that I came down with allergies and a minor head cold. Contracting an illness is certainly an expeditious, though unpleasant, way to learn more about a new culture.

In the process of getting sick, I realized that temperature in Hong Kong is always referenced in Celsius. It took me about a year to adjust to this calibration for weather and baking. But I still preferred Fahrenheit for taking my temperature when I got sick. Who wants to do math while suffering from a fever?

To quote an American friend of mine who used to live in Asia: "Although I understand Celsius, Fahrenheit is my heart language."

When I went in to see a local doctor, I was alarmed to be given at least four or five little zippered plastic bags with different medications. I figured I must be deathly ill for a doctor to prescribe so many pills. While doing an internet search though, I discovered I'd been given a variety of mild tablets for headache, cough, and congestion. None were stronger than what would be over-the-counter meds in America such as Tylenol, Benadryl, and Robitussin.

I also learned on this doctor visit that in Hong Kong a doctor would give me my medications directly and include it in the bill rather than writing a prescription and sending me to a separate pharmacy. The drugs didn't come with any leaflets or original packaging—just the name of the medication and dosage instructions scribbled on the zippered bag. This initially concerned me, but I began to realize that the doctors were prescribing such innocuous remedies I had no need to worry. When they gave me something stronger, such as Advil, they offered further instructions and warnings.

In my early months of living in the city, I noticed two different types of pharmacies: Western and Hong Kong-style. Though physicians distributed medication to their patients, drugstores also sold over-the-counter meds. Western pharmacies generally resembled their American counterparts, though the products themselves were imported from a variety of countries and didn't necessarily contain English on their packaging. Much of the medication came from Europe, so French, German, Italian, or even Arabic labels were included. I once searched widely for Dramamine, a remedy for motion sickness. I finally chose a box inscribed with Chinese characters that had a picture of an airplane on it. It seemed to work fine, so it must have been a good guess.

On another occasion, I discovered a tube of cream that claimed to heal all of the following: Pimples. Rash. Prickly heat. Frostbite. Ringworms. Cuts. Insect bites. Sunburn. Chapped skin. Athlete's foot. Eczema. Minor burns. It could also be used as cosmetic cream and aftershave. Either this was the epitome of exaggerated advertising, or I had stumbled upon a miracle cream. Alas, I didn't buy it.

Hong Kong-style pharmacies, on the other hand, looked more like health food stores. They contained a variety of remedies that were not strictly medicinal but related to overall wellbeing. The practice of Chinese medicine was and is a mystery to me. Yet millennia of usage are behind these remedies, so I'm convinced there must be value in it.

A walk through the average Chinese medicine shop, though, felt more like a scavenger hunt in the forest. Deer antlers. Dried flying-squirrel-looking animals. Birds' nests. An assortment of dehydrated fruits, nuts, and berries. Deceased fish and crawling creatures. Flakes, shavings, powders, flowers and leaves, herbs, and a vast array of other unidentified objects.

As I understand it, patients don't need to eat these items. Instead, they boil various combinations of them in water, strain them, and consume the potion as soup or a hot drink. I confess I've not tried many of these cures.

A friend once related to me that he was eating with local Hong Kong buddies when a gnat landed in his pal's noodles. The guy took the bowl back to the proprietor and asked for a fresh bowl. A few minutes later, that same guy showed my friend items he'd purchased from a Chinese medicine shop to cure a minor ailment—including dried bees he planned to boil and swallow. Boiled bees good, gnats on noodles bad? Perhaps the bees were sterilized to make them safe for consumption, but a gnat carried worldly germs?

I don't know, but I'd prefer to avoid both.

CHAPTER 15

FROST AND FOOTBALL

Some aspects of life remain the same across cultures. For example, as I observed during my first December in Hong Kong, Christmas was just as commercialized as elsewhere in the world. In early November, department stores put up holiday decor, shopping malls displayed various Christmas trees, and PA systems blared yuletide tunes.

Some of the decorations were beautiful. For instance, one shopping center assembled a five-story tree laden with twinkling lights and ornaments. Others were garish. Purple trees—not merely purple decorations, but actual purple plastic trees—abounded, as well as trees with metallic or silver "branches."

The most elegant Christmas array in Hong Kong is in the famed Peninsula Hotel. Year after year, they import a real fir tree nearly twenty feet tall, which is then decked with classic ornaments and tasteful lights. The tree makes the already-gorgeous lobby—which features iconic columns, gilded molding, and posh furnishings—the perfect setting for celebrating the season.

On the afternoon of my first Christmas Eve in the city, I journeyed to this lobby to enjoy a holiday concert by a group of alumni from a local university. A makeshift stage surrounded by a velvet rope was set up near the front door. The audience consisted of those dining in the hotel tearoom as well as guests and visitors meandering through the building.

During the program, some spectators stood near the rope directly in front of the choir and took photos of each other with the choir singing in the background. It was an odd sight—a casually-dressed, grinning guest displaying the obligatory peace sign standing in front of a performing choir whose solemn members were dressed in tuxes and gowns, singing "Carol of the Bells."

That first Christmas, I also noticed holiday decorations remained on display until Chinese New Year, which comes in late January or early February, at which point they slowly morphed into similar decor put up for the lunar holiday. This included ornamented trees, Santa decals on glass doors, flamboyant "Merry Christmas" signs stretched out over a highway, and blinking strands of lights around housing estates.

'Tis the season… still.

***

After the stifling summer weather and a few weeks of a mild fall, I was shocked when a bitter cold set in. During that first winter in Hong Kong, the cool weather, with added humidity combined with a stiff wind from the north, seeped into my bones until I thought I'd never again get warm. It was a valid fear as indoor heating is rarely found in Hong Kong apart from portable electric heaters and radiator-type oil heaters. With thick concrete walls that trap in the damp cold and old windows with poor sealing, indoor temperatures in the winter are often only a few degrees higher than outdoors.

While winter was mercifully short, those weeks of lower temperatures felt endless. When at home, I piled on layers of clothing: multiple pairs of socks, two pairs of pants, numerous shirts, a hat, and scarf. Then I waddled around my flat or stayed huddled under four blankets with a hot-water bottle at my feet. I had a space heater plugged into a long extension cord so I could drag it around my home as I moved from room to room.

Since temperatures in Hong Kong had looked mild, at least on paper, I'd failed to bring sufficient warm clothing when I moved there. After a few nights of shivering, I vowed to dig out my winter clothing from storage when I next traveled to America. I'd never imagined needing long-underwear in a subtropical Southeast Asian climate. After one disastrous incident that involved me simultaneously plugging in three heaters and consequently blowing a fuse, I decided dressing in layers was a safe and wise decision. The record low inside my flat is 47.5° F (8.6° C). Thankfully, I experienced this only once since moving to Hong Kong.

Some years later when the mercury outside crept down to freezing, Hong Kong residents awoke on a Sunday morning to a rare frost warning. The news showed Hong Kongers flooding the hillsides to see icy particles on plants and trees. This created a traffic gridlock and became a dangerous situation as many people had to be rescued from frozen hiking paths after suffering twisted ankles. Emergency personnel couldn't gain access because other icicle seekers jammed the narrow mountainous roads. It seemed that many Hong Kongers had more frosty weather curiosity than frosty weather experience.

***

Super Bowl Sunday is not a true holiday, though I have family members who'd argue with that statement. But during my first winter in Hong Kong, some American friends and I made an attempt to celebrate it as such. As with other non-local holidays, we postponed the festivities to suit our schedules.

The Super Bowl was aired live on a local television station beginning on Monday morning around 7:00 a.m. Hong Kong-time—this, of course, being Sunday evening back in the United States. Different commentators guided local viewers through the game for this special international broadcast.

While American, the commentators assumed the average viewer was not. So for the benefit of spectators who hear the word "football" and picture the sport played with a round white-and-black ball, they explained the rules of this uniquely American game in meticulous detail. As one who barely understood the basics of football while marching in my high school band during halftime, I appreciated this. My male football-enthusiast friends, however, found it mildly irritating.

Because we all had to work on Monday, someone recorded the game that morning while the rest of us went about our normal day. We all took great pains to avoid learning in advance the final outcome of the game. Turning on my computer, I held a large piece of paper over the screen as the internet opened and I carefully maneuvered to my email inbox without looking at anything except the address bar. (This was in the days before social media and streaming services.)

As a co-worker entered my office, I preemptively blurted out, "Good afternoon how are you I haven't seen the game yet please please don't tell me the score sorry thank you!"

Even in unexpected places—the train, for example, where news clips played on television screens—opportunities arose to accidentally overhear the score, spoiling all our efforts. At the end of this taxing day, we gathered in someone's flat and shared the close encounters we'd faced. Inevitably, someone had learned the score already. They were sworn to silence lest they face the punishment of not being allowed to eat the fudge brownies.

I appreciate a good game and a close competition, but I admit I generally care very little who wins and who loses. I'm the ignorant spectator who shows up at the Super Bowl party asking, "Now, which teams are playing?" and remarking, "Okay, I'll root for the ones in the blue uniforms."

Our Super Bowl party was complete with pizza, seven-layer dip, tortilla chips, Oreos, soda, and other artery-clogging classic American junk food. At 5:00 p.m., we were still searching the city for a can of refried beans—an important layer in the dip. By 7:00 p.m., the condiments were assembled, the pizza ordered, and we settled back to poke fun at the performer who flubbed the National Anthem.

Then the game began. We had the freedom to fast-forward through uninteresting portions. The commercials were local and not necessarily in English, so the normally three-to-four-hour game proceeded quickly. Someone paused the recording as we grabbed another slice of pizza or got a refill of ice in our drink. We lampooned the halftime entertainment but sang along with the performers, thoroughly immersed in American culture. The game wrapped up before 10:00 p.m., and we laughed at the fact that we'd managed to watch a game twelve hours after it took place, yet celebrated it as though a live event.

For those few hours, we might have been in someone's spacious living room in the American Midwest on a Sunday afternoon, eating everyday snacks we'd just purchased that weekend at the neighborhood grocery store. Instead, we were sitting in a small flat on the thirty-seventh floor of a high-rise building, eating layered dip that included a US$3 can of refried beans. We munched on pepperoni pizza that had to be specially ordered because it was not on the regular menu and shared one bag of tortilla chips which had been set aside for this important day.

Afterwards, I headed home to watch the best part of the game—those classic commercials on YouTube.

CHAPTER 16

OPERA AND DARTH VADER

Because I worked on Sundays, it wasn't until several months into my time in Hong Kong that I saw firsthand a remarkable phenomenon. Each Sunday, streets and sidewalks around the city teem with domestic helpers who essentially camp out for the day. Because their "home" is in their employer's flat, they go out on their day off. A quarter of a million women need a place to rest and relax for ten to twelve hours, so they fill up parks, public areas, closed streets, shopping malls, and other civic venues.

In Central—the primary business district on Hong Kong-side—an underground walkway designed for pedestrian traffic becomes a bivouac for these women. They spread out sections of cardboard, towels, blankets, or sheets of newspaper on which to sit. Some assemble a pup-tent as protection from the sun and rain. In groups of two or three or ten, they gather in community for socializing, playing games, singing, eating, or napping.

One woman has a T-shirt draped over her face as she catches a snooze. Others hide behind open umbrellas or plastic tarps. Four women engage in a card game, lazily whiling away the time. Others dive into a boxed meal of cold rice, vegetables, and fresh fruit, chatting about their week. A group of twelve create a dance routine to music that plays from a mobile phone while others look on with enjoyment.

Around dusk, the women began to scatter, gathering up their belongings, bidding farewell to one another, and reluctantly returning to their employer's home where they may be expected to clean up from the family's weekend activities. On Sunday evening, the only remaining evidence of this diaspora are piles of cardboard—which ragpickers will later collect and recycle—and rubbish bins overflowing with refuse. Another tiring week has begun for this crowd of hardworking Southeast Asians.

***

Music of all kinds can be heard among the Filipino community as they spread out around the city on weekends. Not Cantonese opera, though. I mostly hear this unique genre of music on the radio when riding public transportation.

High-pitched, lilting melodies are sung in a nasal voice. The haunting tunes resemble heightened speaking—*recitative*-like at times and at other moments like pentatonic melodies with unexpected leaps. Though clear-cut phrases feel absent, a steady duple meter maintains continuity. Percussive instruments—woodblocks and rhythm sticks—provide sound effects in the background. A countermelody played on an *erhu*, a traditional Chinese stringed instrument, adds texture and an occasional sense of harmony to the piece. A gong signals the ending of one section and the elided beginning of the next. This is Cantonese opera.

My most memorable experience with this Hong Kong art form occurred at a concert in my church given by Mr. and Mrs. Man, the uncle and aunt of a friend of mine. This husband-wife duo were highly talented and well-known Cantonese opera singers who had performed worldwide. Though originally Buddhist, later in life they became committed Christians.

Historically, most professional Cantonese opera singers earned the majority of their income by participating in ritual performances. Village residents hosted such presentations to celebrate the birthdays of gods, to ensure good luck, or to gain protection from evil spirits. Mr. and Mrs. Man had already invested more than five decades in the pursuit of Cantonese opera and didn't want to abandon their career.

Upon becoming Christians, though, they were unwilling to keep participating in these religious rites associated with local temples and gods. Eventually, they began writing Cantonese opera songs that told stories from the Bible. Thus, they were able to continue their pursuit of this music, albeit with different audiences.

The concert I attended consisted of the Mans singing their own Cantonese opera music without the dramatic acting, props, or acrobatics common to this genre. As an art form, I find Cantonese opera fascinating—learning about the standardized roles with accompanying costumes and makeup, or the bamboo theaters in which performances historically took place. But I've never gotten used to the jarring sounds and lack of harmonic resolution. Being able to enjoy this style of music, especially when blaring over the radio in a bus or taxi, must be a taste I haven't yet acquired. Nevertheless, I appreciated this particular concert because of its cultural value, and I knew the music and its message were meaningful to the attendees.

***

Effective communication is challenging in any culture, and much more so when mixing cultures. Perusal of tips for American businesspeople who plan to work with Asian companies reveals several key differences in communication styles. Asians place such high value on social harmony that the importance of group cohesion often supersedes the need for resolution. Relationships, human connections, and business contacts are valuable, perhaps more so than agendas.

On the flip side, Americans—ever the individualists—express personal opinions freely and directly with the goal of persuading others to agree. They work toward the end result in the quickest way possible, regardless of how others feel or react.

A meeting in Hong Kong may begin late, open with much chitchat, and proceed in a circuitous fashion. Attendees may weave between addressing matters of business and speculating on unrelated issues. I attended one such meeting, for example, in which we covered the topics on our agenda as well as the local economy, gangs, and drug-runners in Hong Kong. Additionally, attendees talked through the politics of Singapore, the weather of Houston, the dubious benefits of meeting people at Lan Kwai Fong (an area of Hong Kong known for its pubs), and the flats in Hong Kong that seem "designed for Pygmies" (their words, not mine). It was an enlightening few hours for me.

In these situations, I sometimes feel frustrated with the lack of focus. I would prefer to jump in and tackle issues head on, whereas Asians loop around the issue, coming back to it at various points in the conversation. Problems may not be addressed directly, but rather in an oblique manner. If a particularly serious topic is on the table, there may be long moments of silence as people digest information. Silence in a meeting is disconcerting to Westerners like me, but not necessarily uncomfortable for Asians.

An interesting side note: when Americans speak of "tabling an issue," they mean that it should be saved for a later discussion.

British English speakers—and, thus, Hong Kongers—use the phrase to mean the opposite. A topic is "tabled," or put on the table, to be discussed now.

It is not unheard of for a meeting in Hong Kong to adjourn when attendees reach a unanimous decision on an issue, only to discover later that members actually disagreed with one another but didn't wish to express their dissent in front of the group. This scenario is the result of "saving face." Americans also use the idiom "save face," but I find that this concept is more deeply ingrained in Asian culture.

Simply put, saving face means "to avoid having other people lose respect for oneself."[11] In the West, there is a preference for people to tell the truth and be brutally honest. For many Asians, this is distasteful. Social harmony and the reputation of individuals take precedence over the need for complete transparency or accuracy. Mistakes should not be pointed out, and disagreements ought to be avoided or smoothed over.

Social ranking is also important to group dynamics in Hong Kong. Many times, participants of a meeting will defer to senior members before speaking up. Hierarchy within organizations and companies in Asia is clear and known to all employees. Members should never question authority or attempt to skip over the level immediately above them. Top-down leadership styles are most common, and workers adhere to the boss's verdict.

Contrast this with America, where people favor egalitarian interactions and value equality among employees or members of a social group. The boss has the final say, but other personnel expect

[11] *Merriam-Webster,* s.v. "save face (idiom)," accessed January 25, 2018, https://www.merriam-webster.com/dictionary/save%20face.

to have their ideas and opinions heard. Decisions are frequently collaborative.

Of course, all these cultural mannerisms are generalizations and oversimplifications. Asia, the most populous continent, encompasses so many different people groups that it is absurd to characterize them by one set of behavioral traits. Even when speaking of Chinese people, there are vast differences among Hong Kong Chinese, Mainland Chinese, Singapore Chinese, Taiwan Chinese, American-born Chinese, Canadian-born Chinese, and Australian-born Chinese. Likewise, large disparities exist among Westerners. My friends from the American Midwest prefer not to be mixed up with the crazy Texans, for instance, and I'd rather not be mistaken for a Yankee.

***

My favorite language phenomenon in Hong Kong is *Chinglish*—a unique combination of English and Cantonese that occurs when the languages emerge together, often within the same sentence. Because of Hong Kong's history as a British colony and the international character of the city, some words don't have a Cantonese translation. In such cases, the English term remains in everyday usage.

This creative method of communication—which has parallels with other language combinations around the world, such as Spanglish in the United States—is a way to converse easily without either language causing a limitation. It's like having two options for every word with the ability to choose the better one. Hong Kongers refer to this as "changing channels," meaning they quickly swap from one language to another depending on the conversation participants and topic of discussion.

An example of this coexistence is the Cantonese phrase for "relax," as a photographer would say to a person posing for a picture or a doctor would say to a patient who's ready for an injection. If written in *pinyin*, it is "*fong sung* D" with the letter "D" pronounced just like it sounds and meaning "a little bit more." The capitalized letter "D" would actually be printed alongside the Chinese characters, even in a non-English, non-*pinyin* context.

In my first year of living in Hong Kong, a local friend and I went to a steakhouse for dinner. She ordered both our meals in Cantonese until it was time to clarify the cooking of the meat. "Well done" and "rare" were spoken in English by both my friend and the waiter.

When I asked her about this later, she shrugged and said, "The English terms are understood by everyone, so there's no common Cantonese translation."

Makes sense, especially since ribeye is not a traditional Chinese meal. Perhaps that is also why an American friend of mine, who was dining in a Chinese/Western fusion restaurant, received an unexpected surprise when she ordered steak with "gravy on the side." Due to the failure of idiomatic translation, she literally got gravy on the side—i.e., gravy on only *half* of her meat.

In a more recent experience involving Chinglish, I viewed a live Star Wars performance at the Hong Kong Disneyland in which the actors onstage, who happened to be Jedi, spoke Cantonese. Darth Vader—whose voice was pre-recorded and came with a variety of background sound effects—spoke English. In this case, it was easy to distinguish between the light side and the dark side.

CHAPTER 17

KINFOLK AND PINWHEELS

Chinese New Year. It is known as the largest mass movement of humanity at any one point in time. A quarter of the world's population celebrates. Most businesses close for the week. Students are on vacation for a fortnight. Flights are booked solid, and public transportation is packed as people journey to spend time with family.

Nothing could have prepared me for this holiday that first year I lived in Hong Kong. Combine all of the American celebrations of Thanksgiving, Christmas, and New Year's into one, and this only begins to approach the enormity of the Chinese New Year (CNY) holiday in Asia. This colossal celebration lasted several weeks in ancient times. In Hong Kong it has been reduced to three public holidays to accommodate capitalistic endeavors. But across Asia and by Chinese people worldwide, it still functions as the focal point of the year.

CNY—also called the Lunar New Year—starts on the first day of the first month of the lunar calendar. In the Western Gregorian calendar, this can fall anywhere from January 22 to February 20. On the eve of CNY, celebrants set off firecrackers, ostensibly to scare away bad luck and evil spirits. Certain family members must be visited on particular days of the New Year holiday, beginning with the most senior relatives on the husband's side.

On the second day, a family will typically visit the wife's parents. The common custom for the third day is to stay home to avoid quarreling or arguing with extended family. After a few days of celebration with kinfolk, perhaps it is indeed wise to hunker down and give everyone a familial break. (I'm speaking rhetorically, of course, with no reference to my own family.)

Initially, I was confused when people gave me gifts during the CNY season. After all, what to me was the gift-giving season, Christmas, was already over. I soon learned that sharing generously with others—friends, visiting guests, coworkers, and family—is part of the CNY celebration. Gifts of candy and fruit symbolically wish good luck and a sweet year ahead for the receiver. People also give tea, snacks, potted flowers, and healthcare products.

From the first official day of CNY and throughout the following weeks, married couples give out red packets—typically a small red envelope embellished with a flowery design or gold calligraphy—containing cash. The bills inside, which are crisp and new, should be in certain denominations, always ending in an even number but without including a four (such as forty, four hundred, etc.), as the number four suggests bad luck. Packets are given to children and young single adults, as well as people in service positions such as waiters, building workers, housekeepers, and other employees. As a young single adult, I quickly decided this was a new tradition I could embrace.

Many other CNY-related customs I learned about—words you should refrain from saying, gifts that shouldn't be given, actions to avoid, ways to ensure good luck or dodge bad luck—were traditional but not widely observed. Hong Kongers may have a general knowledge of these practices but often place little validity in them. CNY celebrations in the big cities have become commercialized and urbanized. Work schedules and travel timetables dictate family visits. Gifts are often more practical than symbolic. Fireworks are enjoyed for their spectacular display rather than for any religious significance. And, thankfully, Hong Kongers are merciful toward foreigners like me who frequently, if inadvertently, "break the rules" by saying or doing the wrong thing at the wrong time.

***

In the weeks before CNY, open-air flower markets are organized in several areas throughout Hong Kong, filled with fresh green plants, flowers, fruit, trinkets, and souvenirs reflecting both the local culture and the holiday. I was excited on my first CNY when one of my new local friends offered to take me to this celebratory display. Wall-to-wall people crowded around each stall, surveying the goods and jostling one another in an effort to see what was available.

The most common purchase seemed to be flowers. There were long-stemmed purple or pink blossoms in porcelain vases. Plants grown in shapes that resembled various animals with bright red ribbons adorning each item. Bamboo plants in a myriad of shapes and sizes. Colorful orchids, daisies, peach blossoms, jasmine, lilies, chrysanthemums, narcissus, and more. The array of flowers was truly astonishing, not to mention the sheer number of miniature mandarin orange and tangerine trees.

Knickknacks also abounded. Balloon animals. Toy figurines. Inflatable creatures of all shapes. Bright paper decorations. Noisemakers. Paper wall hangings.

Though the throngs of people felt overwhelming at times, I loved the excitement and spirit of merriment as families and friends strolled around together. This was the place to buy any kind of plush toy. There were animals—especially whatever animal corresponded to that year of the Chinese zodiac. Bugs. Popular cartoon characters. Alien-looking creatures. A carrot. Hello Kitty. A lantern. Even a basket of dim sum. All made of fabric with stuffing inside.

One young woman wearing an *E.T.* sweatshirt demonstrated a handmade paper dragon marionette. Vendors sold novelties constructed of fake money—both Hong Kong bills and American—though customers had to use legitimate cash to purchase them. I enjoyed tasting the goodies. Roasted nuts. Sweet bars made of sesame seeds. Coconut candy. And a host of other snacks for which I didn't know the names.

Later that evening, I eyed some handmade pinwheels consisting of a dowel rod with delicate, colorful paper strips twisted and attached to the plastic wheel. A small red flag secured to the tip offered a token phrase of good fortune or wish for long life. The child in me emerged, and I paid about US$2 for the bauble. Only later did I realize that this object was commonly associated with fortunetelling. I took it home and stored it in a closet, almost forgotten.

Several years later, this pinwheel came in handy when I was taking care of my baby godson. He began sobbing when his parents left, and the pinwheel proved to be the only thing that distracted him enough to stop crying. I guess the toy brought good luck after all.

CHAPTER 18

DRAGONS AND FIRE

Some refer to Hong Kong as "Asia's World City." Nothing demonstrated this more than the parade I saw that first Chinese New Year (CNY) I lived in Hong Kong. My friends took me to a major street on Hong Kong-side where we could view this spectacle. Entrants represented countries from all over the world. Marching bands playing lively tunes and energizing the crowd reminded me of my own high school marching band experience. The parade featured giant inflatable oceanic creatures, symbolic of the local theme park, competing with Donald Duck and friends on the Hong Kong Disneyland float.

Theatrical entertainers walked on stilts, waving flags and wearing colorful garb. Tribal groups clad in indigenous clothing beat authentic hand-drums or other percussion instruments. Dance troupes, dressed in shimmering costumes, performed their choreographed routines. A large float complete with horses and riders represented the Hong Kong Jockey Club. Mascots from far away sports teams marched along, including that of the Texan football team, which surprised me.

A group of Asian men played large, deep-sounding drums while simultaneously whirling their necks. Hats perched atop their heads, onto which a swivel was attached, allowed them to twirl tassels in a synchronized routine. I knew from experience how hard it was to play a musical instrument while marching in sync. I couldn't imagine having to add a spinning headpiece.

The parade included the classic dragon dance, which consisted of people wearing oversized, colorful dragon heads moving to a rhythmic beat. Other skilled entertainers, also dressed in large dragon costumes, balanced atop fifteen-foot poles, moving to the distinctly Chinese music as their forefathers had for centuries. Kids from all over the globe danced, marched, and frolicked down the streets in their cultural costumes, waving, grinning shyly, and clearly enjoying the attention. Children are children all the world over.

This parade exemplified what I've come to love most about Hong Kong. I didn't need to travel the earth when the nations of the world came here. And it was especially fun when those nations brought their festive clothing and unique traditions, putting them on display in a spirited holiday procession.

***

On the second or third day of Chinese New Year, Hong Kong presents a multi-million-dollar, awe-inspiring fireworks display over Victoria Harbour—one of my favorite events of any holiday. About half a million ooohing and aaahing fans gather annually to watch this brilliant exhibit of pyrotechnics, some arriving as many as eight hours early to secure a front row seat. The sacrifice is great, but the reward is worth it.

Friends had invited me to attend the CNY fireworks show with them, so we met together mid-afternoon at a spot near the

Kowloon-side waterfront. Photographers—both professional and amateurs—had set up their tripods, anchoring them to the railing on the water's edge, hoping to capture this quintessential Asian extravaganza. More people began to arrive in small groups later in the afternoon, all scouting a place to sit.

A grandstand was already full, and the photographers had taken over the oceanfront. But there remained many large areas of unreserved empty space. Families spread out newspaper, sheets of plastic, or cardboard on which to sit. Youth gathered in groups, playing games or chatting, their laughter floating through the air. Small children slept in strollers or in the arms of parents.

I enjoyed this microcosm of life as my friends and I lounged on an old sheet. It felt like we were at a picnic or outdoor fair. We pulled out a deck of cards, shared the snacks we'd brought, then took turns visiting the nearby shopping center to utilize the restrooms.

This trek was a feat in itself, involving stepping over throngs of people, threading around picnic blankets and camera tripods, and searching for a gap in the crowd. I decided to limit my liquid intake.

As the hours wore on, the area became more densely packed. It was impossible to leave by then, though police labored to maintain open passageways for emergency exits. Dusk descended, and people grew restless. As some stood to stretch their legs, the multitude abruptly began pressing forward in a solid mass. Though it was a peaceful movement, I felt claustrophobic. A wide stance, thrust-out elbows, and a bulging backpack helped create a small bubble of personal space around me.

Promptly at 8:00 p.m., music burst forth from the overhead speakers, announcing the start of the long-awaited event. The crowd shoved forward even more, and small children squirmed through the legs of both humans and tripods to stand in the front. At the first explosion, the serene atmosphere suddenly changed into one of noisy delight. This was a participatory event. Onlookers excitedly exclaimed after each eruption of sparks, commenting on the size, color, and variety of the show.

Synchronized fireworks were launched from several barges situated in the middle of the harbor. These cast bright reflections on the water's surface, illuminated the buildings in the background, and lit up faces in the crowd. Colorful laser beams from the skyscrapers pierced through the smoke and clouds from time to time, adding to the flash and spectacle.

Each portion of the visual show was choreographed precisely to music. A classical piece by Strauss. An Asian pop song. A Chinese opera aria. The national anthem and more. As a musician, I especially enjoyed this aspect of the event.

Still, it was hard to discern my feelings in that moment. Were the fireworks meaningful to me because they called to mind America and my childhood experiences on the Fourth of July? Was the magic due to the sense of unity found among a mass of people all gathered for the same thrilling experience? Or perhaps I was stirred for the mundane reason that fireworks in general are impressive, and these were the best of the best, presented by descendants of the very inventors of pyrotechnic displays. Or maybe I just liked fire set to music.

After twenty minutes, the show drew to a close. People began to gather their belongings. Photographers captured final shots. Chatter rose as the throng of humanity gradually dispersed. The walk back to the train station was a long journey, due to the sheer size of the slowly moving crowd. As we shuffled along, a reporter from a local television network approached me to ask what I thought about the show.

Eyeing the microphone in my face, cameraman, and news crew, I immediately grew tongue-tied and indicated she should interview my friends. I also felt slightly annoyed she'd singled me out. Thousands of Hong Kongers surrounded us, but she'd presumably chosen me because of my pointy nose and Western face. I would later learn this happens often to foreigners in Hong Kong.

I didn't speak to the newswoman that night, but as I inched toward the train, I thought back over the impressive ending of the show. The grand finale had lasted over sixty seconds as the remainder of the fireworks were launched in immediate succession, creating an unparalleled display of sights and sounds. The glistening water below caught the brilliance. The entire sky was lit with color. As the music crescendoed, the crowd's energy continued to rise. But the deafening explosions bouncing from one side of the harbor to the other obscured all ambient sound.

Then a final flash of light, one last thundering boom that shook the ground, and it was over. The multitude cheered and clapped heartily as embers floated through the smoky sky. A dense cloud of haze hung lazily over the harbor, temporarily concealing the backdrop of city lights and skyscrapers. A sudden calm rang through the air.

Another Lunar New Year had opened with a spectacular bang.

CHAPTER 19

TRUMPETS AND MARSHMALLOWS

One night not long after moving to Hong Kong, I was sitting in my home when I heard a neighbor woman singing opera music—Western-style opera. An ethereal melody, almost haunting, it echoed among the buildings, occasionally punctuated by a tenor voice with full vibrato. I was transported to starlit Venice, mentally serenaded down the Grand Canal in a gondola.

Another evening, I spent several excruciating hours suffering through a beginner trumpeter's rudimentary exercises coming from a neighbor's flat. Considering the length of practice and repetitive yet basic nature of the playing, I suspected the student was cramming for a lesson or class. Side note to beginning musicians: cramming cannot replace daily instrumental practice.

One day after months of hearing this slowly progressing trumpeter, I looked across at the next building and realized the musician was an elderly gentleman. Applauding his efforts, I stopped allowing the din to bother me. On yet another evening, I sat on my sofa trying to determine what instrument I was hearing from elsewhere in the building. I concluded it was a plastic recorder played by a non-musician.

Piano students thrive in Hong Kong, and it's not uncommon to hear scales practiced late into the night along with strains of Bach, Chopin, or Mozart. Brass instruments and piano music are, in my opinion, generally preferable over the beginner woodwind. Pity the neighborhood where a Grade 1 clarinetist or oboist resides. The squeaks and squawks of a reed instrument can make one cringe. Stringed instruments—equally popular to the piano in this city—can also create the sensation of fingernails on the chalkboard when a student is learning fundamentals.

The sounds of music—mismatched timbres, wrong notes, and poor intonation aside—are oddly soothing to me, likely because of the years I've spent studying music. Standing in a crowded high school band hall surrounded by sixty other instrumentalists, each playing their own melodies and rhythms at once, creates a unique atmosphere. Tonalities mix and pitches clash as one walks down the practice room hallways of the college music building. A pianist here, a vocalist there. Familiar tunes and new refrains blend. Together, a new kind of music is created.

That's what I hear in my neighborhood. Yes, there are times I'd like to open my window and hear the silence of the night punctuated gently by the song of crickets and croaking of frogs, sounds of my childhood home backyard. But as a professional musician who believes in teaching music to children and adults of all ages, I am grateful to know that my neighbors are hard at work improving their musical skills.

So when I open my bedroom window and hear "Three Blind Mice" breathily played on the penny whistle—or maybe it's that plastic recorder—I smile to myself. Music is in the air.

***

"Too close to fire. It will burn."

I sat around a barbecue pit, surrounded by half-a-dozen elderly Chinese women, receiving instructions on how to roast a hotdog over a campfire. Several hundred of us had gathered at a park, which we'd rented for a daylong church outing in which the focal point was the barbecue. We'd been divided into two large groups, and each group had been sent to a particular section of the park. I was told to meet at Pit B.

Pit B consisted of twenty or so small barbecue pits built of concrete, permanently affixed to the ground and surrounded by cement benches. I was standing there alone, surveying the area, when a woman grabbed my arm and urged me to sit with her group, which consisted of elderly Cantonese-speaking women.

Well, if I'm attending an authentic Hong Kong barbecue, I told myself, it ought to be experienced with locals.

Thankfully, everyone was wearing nametags. I introduced myself, and one woman told me which individuals could speak some English. I worried that my presence would bother them. In my experience, Cantonese speakers who don't know English often feel uncomfortable around an English-only speaker. But they seemed pleased I'd joined them. I soon had them rolling with laughter as I attempted to pronounce some Cantonese words and entertained them with the few Chinese idioms I knew.

Meanwhile, plastic bags of charcoal had been delivered to each campfire, and various men from our church group set out to build fires. Hong Kong charcoal doesn't come in uniform square briquettes, but in different sizes and shapes. Those who arranged the charcoal in each pit donned cheap fabric gloves as they extracted the blackened chunks from the bag. When it comes to building a fire, it seems all cultures are the same. The menfolk stand around debating the best way to arrange the charcoal and kindling, each studying the situation and offering different opinions before finally actually lighting the fire.

No lighter fluid was used, but each campfire received a box of nuggets consisting of some kind of flammable material. Stacks of newspaper were also distributed. Soon, paper-waving people surrounded each pit while bits of ash and flakes of newsprint floated down from the sky. I stepped away from the smoke, covering my mouth with a tissue, as I noted how many dark-haired Asians now had gray paper fragments on their heads. Organic kindling—twigs and small sticks—would have been better for the environment and my lungs as well. But I kept my mouth shut.

Eventually, the fires grew, and the remaining newspapers were spread out at our feet. I was handed one thin disposable glove, a long metal barbecue fork, and a resealable bag filled with pieces of raw meat soaking in blood. My stomach turned as I realized the glove was for pulling out pieces of drippy meat and placing them on the fork for roasting. I was accustomed to barbecuing only precooked meat, i.e., hotdogs, or placing raw meat like hamburger patties on a strip of tin foil or metal barbecue tray. Perhaps I should consider vegetarianism.

Gingerly pulling out the only hotdog in my bag, I placed it on the skewer. The others opted for raw chicken wings or thin slabs of pink pork. I did my best to get into the spirit of the moment. But in my mind I was seeing red flags waving, on which were written words such as salmonella and *E. coli*. My solution was to overcook the meat, which caused the Chinese grandmas to fuss at me. "Don't hold it so close to the fire. You're burning it!"

I actually didn't mind the crunchy, charred meat, but my new friends warned me I shouldn't eat it. We'd each been handed plastic non-disposable plates, but they looked poorly washed. So I chose the germ-free option of eating the frankfurter directly off the hot metal skewer, prompting more admonishments from the grandmas.

Next, I picked up the only other pre-cooked meat in my baggie: two very small sausage-looking items. As I placed the tiny bits on my barbecue fork, I was criticized for wasting space on the skewer. After all, several chunks of meat could have fit on it at once. This time I relinquished my desire to eat the mini sausages straight off the hot fork. Instead, I tried to slide them onto my plate—quite a feat since one hand still wore a glove covered in raw meat juice. Unfortunately, the tiny sausages rolled off onto the ground before I could get them into my mouth.

Since there was nothing else in my meat baggie I wished to eat, I then tried to roast a few dim sum fish balls. These are a favorite among Hong Kongers and a snack I usually enjoy. But the selections provided were rather low-quality. Why couldn't *they* have rolled onto the ground instead?

Then I spied a box of fresh apples nearby. These, along with slices of white bread and a few ears of corn, were the only non-meat items offered. I surreptitiously offered my bag of bloody chicken and pork to a teenager at the next barbecue pit, then eagerly devoured an apple.

While eating, I conversed with the woman next to me, commenting that I wished we had marshmallows to roast. She didn't understand what I was talking about, so I began to describe a marshmallow, a task I'd never undertaken before. It's small and white-colored. Made mostly of sugar, soft and squishy. When it gets hot, the inside melts. Her face finally lit up, and she said a word in Cantonese.

"Yes, that's it," I responded, as if I knew what she was saying.

Meanwhile, I continued to fend off questions from the Chinese grandmas. "Why are you not eating more?... Surely you're not full yet?"

At last, it was time for me to depart for home. There I would enjoy a satisfying, fully cooked lunchmeat sandwich followed by a bit of chocolate.

In my growing-up experience, much of my family preferred to live remotely from our food's origins. We would eat meat but not admit it actually came from a living creature. If it arrived in our kitchen in a can or package, or pre-cooked and frozen, so much the better. My city-bred mother had a rule at the dinner table: no mention of living beasts or meat sources while eating. Our innocent childhood questions—"Is this pig or cow?"—as we held a forkful of grilled meat aloft were curtailed.

I still prefer it that way. Boneless, skinless, headless, feet-less, bloodless, and deveined, please. And note to self: next time I attend a Hong Kong barbecue, I'll bring the marshmallows.

CHAPTER 20

PIGS AND KARAOKE

Few events are more impressive than a Chinese wedding banquet. It's like stepping into a fairy tale where we can forget our ordinary existence for a few hours until we walk outside at the end of a long night.

On one warm evening, I found myself in a crowded restaurant banquet hall celebrating the wedding of two friends. The banquet was a typical Hong Kong affair: loud, colorful, and packed with tradition. Round tables filled the room, each one containing a lazy Susan, a decorative centerpiece, and a printed list of the dinner courses to be served—usually about twelve. Hong Kongers consider the wedding banquet of utmost importance, perhaps more so than the actual ceremony.

As guests entered, they had their photograph taken with the happy couple on a makeshift stage at one end of the hall. The bride wore an elaborate red dress, which looked fit for a royal ball though it inhibited movement or sitting. Throughout the evening, the bride and groom intermittently left and re-entered the room, dressed in different attire each time. Customarily, a bride would start out wearing a red dress—the traditional color for a Chinese wedding—

followed by a Western-style white gown with a flowing train, then change into different colored dresses.

Prior to dinner, waiters and waitresses milled around distributing drinks. Most Hong Kong banquets—wedding or otherwise—serve the same choice of non-alcoholic beverages: hot tea and water, colas, and orange juice. Always orange juice. Why not other flavors of juice? I love orange juice, but I find it doesn't pair well with crab cakes or choi sum.

Partway through the evening, the newlyweds cut the ceremonial wedding cake, a delectable-looking confection that wasn't edible. It was a plastic replica with a special slot hidden in the back into which a knife was inserted for a photographic moment. We enjoyed dessert later, but it didn't include cake. The cake ceremony was a nod to Western wedding traditions, which had become common during British rule, while acknowledging that many Hong Kongers don't enjoy overly sweet desserts.

As the dinner courses began, there was much discussion about the various foods. Five minutes passed in which everyone at my table weighed in with their idea of what a "fish maw" was, as it was listed on the menu.

"I think it's the mouth of the fish," said one.

"The fish's cheek?" asked another.

I wondered if it was akin to a paw, but fish don't have paws. Could it just be a mistranslation of some other body part? When I arrived home later, I looked up the term and discovered it referred to the mouth, throat, or gullet of an animal. It can also mean a cavernous opening resembling the jaws of an animal, as in the gaping *maw* of hell. I'm not entirely sure what we ate that night.

A climactic moment of any Chinese banquet with multiple courses is the suckling pig. No need to label it pork. This is a whole pig, head and all, delivered to the table. Waiters, holding platters overhead exhibiting said pigs, paraded into the room one after the other while the "Mickey Mouse March" music blared over the PA system—a startlingly sprightly tune to signal the demise of a barbecued swine.

We were given one glance at the pig, and then it was whisked away to the kitchen. The music faded, and waiters began serving delicious bits of crispy pork skin and fatty meat slices. The turnaround was so fast this food couldn't possibly have come from the same animals that had entered just a few minutes earlier.

Other typical wedding banquet courses followed. Shrimp balls. Whelk and mushrooms. Snow peas and scallops. Seafood and melon soup. Bak choi. Whole steamed fish. Cantonese-style roasted chicken. Noodles and fried rice. The newlyweds changed clothing several more times, and all guests gathered onstage for photos again, group by group and as individuals.

There were two emcees—a male and female—to keep events moving. They read scripted lines of humor, introduced special guests, presented slideshows and videos, and translated every comment and announcement into both Cantonese and English. We saw childhood photos, engagement photos, wedding photos from the church ceremony that morning, and a recap of the entire day.

There is an enormous amount of activity and tradition expected of the bride and groom on this day. Bridesmaids—already attired in their wedding finery and makeup—appeared at the bride's door around 4:00 a.m. that morning, dragging her out to complete a multitude of "tasks," which were like a freshman hazing or bridal shower games. The groomsmen and groom conducted similar activities early in the morning.

Then it was time for the whole wedding party to undertake more serious rituals. Traditional breakfasts. Exchanging gifts with important family members. Paying homage to senior relatives. And of course, the requisite tea ceremony. This latter rite involved the couple bowing before the bride's parents, then later the groom's parents, and serving hot tea to them on bended knee. The two sets of parents bestowed a gift on the couple, along with blessings for a profitable future.

The four-hour long banquet concluded with dessert, which included a choice of coconut or sweet red-bean soup and squares of jellied Osmanthus flowers with goji berries. I arose from the table feeling like I'd indulged in a Thanksgiving feast and vowing never to eat again. Still, the American in me wished there'd been cake.

* * *

At another wedding I attended years later, the crowning touch of the evening came when I and two other non-Chinese-speakers were invited onstage for an audience participation game. We each took a turn donning earphones to an MP3 player on which a Canto-pop love song played. While listening to the song in the headphones, we had to sing what we heard into a microphone to a large, boisterous Cantonese-speaking audience. The goal was for an audience member to name the song, thereby winning a prize. They called it "guess that tune." My dad suggested it be called "karaoke-charades."

I don't know who won the game, but it certainly wasn't me.

* * *

I once completed an online survey for a local Hong Kong company, after being lured in by the chance to win a bookstore gift card. In the section collecting personal information, one question read: How would you describe your marital status?

1. Married

2. Single

3. Other

4. Refused

What does "refused" mean in this context? One who has refused marriage? One who was refused, as in a rejected marriage proposal? Unrequited love?

Subsequent questions on other topics offered the same choice, which led me to believe it actually meant, "I'd rather not say."

On other Hong Kong government forms I've filled out, the choices given include "refused" and "spinster." Which box would I prefer to check? I'd rather not say.

CHAPTER 21

FRACTIONS AND MAZES

A favorite pastime of mine is perusing the weather forecasts from the Hong Kong Observatory. They fall into the genre of light, humorous reading because they provide such delightful descriptions of weather phenomenon. Here are some of my favorites:

The Very Hot Weather Warning is now in force. Hot weather might cause adverse health effects. Members of the public should take care to avoid heatstroke. (I suppose the capital letters indicate the proper name of the warning. But to me, they emphasize the severity of the issue, i.e., it will be Very Hot!")

The weather will be appreciably cooler in the coming days. ("Appreciably cooler" seems a bit subjective, but it is true that I'm grateful for less heat.)

There will be one or two rain patches today. (This is surprisingly specific compared to the vaguer North American weather reports, which would say "scattered showers.")

Some weather reports include cheerful suggestions:

The weather will become cold progressively in the next few days. Please get prepared and put on warm clothes. (In case the drop in temperature itself didn't already prompt people to dress warmly.)

As Hong Kong is being affected by a cold winter monsoon, people are advised to put on warm clothes... If you know of elderly persons or persons with chronic medical conditions staying alone, please call or visit them occasionally to check if they need any assistance. Make sure heaters are safe before use... Do not light fires indoors as a means to keep warm. (In this entry, the information goes beyond the weather report to include individual directives and societal responsibilities.)

At other times, the Observatory posts such confusing forecasts I have to dig deeper into their website for explanation. One frequent weather designation in the fall is "mainly fine and dry." Dry is self-explanatory—the humidity will drop below 80%, I hope—but what exactly is the meaning of "fine" here? The Observatory's page of definitions explains the term:

> *The sky is covered by a total cloud amount of less than six eighths. However, it can still be described as fine even though the total cloud amount is greater than six eighths if the cloud layer is thin enough to let plenty of sunshine to penetrate.*[12]

My math skills involving fractions are poor, so I don't quite comprehend this weather explanation (though shouldn't six eighths be reduced to three fourths?). Still, I know enough to prefer "mainly fine and dry conditions" over Very Hot Weather when I go out to run errands.

[12] "Definitions," Hong Kong Observatory, accessed May 24, 2018, http://www.hko.gov.hk/wxinfo/currwx/flw_description/flw_e.htm#00011.

***

I'd never shopped at an IKEA before moving to Hong Kong, and I wasn't entirely sure what kind of store it was. But within my first month in the city, many people suggested I look there for furniture, curtains, and other household items. So one evening after work, I headed off to the nearest IKEA.

Anyone who has ever shopped at IKEA knows that the marketing scheme employed by this home furnishings giant is a veritable maze. I've always thought of myself as having a solid sense of direction. But in IKEA, I had to keep my eyes trained on the floor, searching for those tiny arrows embedded in the tile to know which direction to go. If I stopped to look at one of the "rooms," I inevitably got turned around. Pretending to study a wall hanging, I was actually eyeing the flow of traffic to determine the proper route.

This labyrinth of merchandise is quite an effective ploy for IKEA. Any time I saw something I might be interested in purchasing, I tended to pick it up. After all, who knew if I'd ever find my way back to it. Even if I thought I could find it again, once I arrived at the exit, I'd be too weary to retrace my steps. So I'd better put it in my cart now, just in case.

I once saw a comedy sketch on television in America back in the early heydays of Super Wal-Mart in which employees of such a store stood at the entrance, welcoming customers. The greeters offered water bottles and maps to those about to embark on a trek through the endless jumble of canned goods, camping equipment, T-shirts, and tires. An apt illustration of the despair and befuddlement I felt when entering an IKEA. Those golf pencils and paper rulers they distribute for free don't offer much comfort. Where is a GPS device when you need it?

My main goal that day was to look at curtains. Arriving at that department, I sought an IKEA staff member and began to traverse the difficult terrain of choosing drapes. I was excited to discover I could hire someone to come measure my windows. This would be no easy task in my flat since each window was a different size, shape, and placement on the wall. Not to mention the air-conditioner window units situated in the middle of the glass panes. An added bonus: choosing this option would allow me to delay the final fabric and color-scheme decisions until later.

At some point while looking at curtain fabric, I became aware of the music playing over the PA system. It was a love ballad sung by a baritone. The lyrics spoke of "staying in one another's arms because that's where we belong" and "we were meant to be together." I'd never heard the song before, but it sounded like something that would be popular in the 1940s. I imagined an old-timey wooden radio with metal knobs nestled in a credenza in a dimly-lit room adorned with ashtrays, shag carpet, and shaded lamps.

Holding up a small curtain rod, I measured it against my arm, trying to remember how wide my bathroom window was. Why hadn't I thought to write down any dimensions before I came? While doing so, I subconsciously noticed that the song had changed keys—again.

"I feel like I've heard this part already," I mused, distracted with the spring-loaded options on curtain rods.

As the drapery section morphed into rugs, I heard the same crooner singing about his lover. Living-rooms became bathrooms, and I realized the song had repeated—there's that modulation again. As I studied the mirror selection, I smiled to myself. Someone had accidentally hit the "repeat one" button on the CD player instead of the "repeat all" button. I was so preoccupied with the music I had to retrace my steps—oh, danger!—to look at the mirrors again.

Office supplies and desks came next. By this time, my grin had faded. Had any IKEA employee even noticed the repetitive song situation? Knick-knacks and picture frames followed. As I scrawled frame measurements on a scrap of paper, my writing became large and loopy as though I was going insane.

I began looking around at my fellow shoppers. One small child was mouthing the words to the song—no doubt learned in the past half-hour. But no one else seemed aware of the circumstances rapidly triggering my mental demise. Wildly, I sought an IKEA salesperson. Alas, they all seemed immersed in conversation with customers. There were some hammers back in the shelf unit section, I reminded myself. Sadly, I couldn't locate a speaker or CD player on which to use one.

By the time I arrived at the bargain section near the checkout area, I felt the song seeping through my insides, tearing at my mind, ripping at my nerves. *If I have to hear the baritone sing that melodramatic modulation one more time...* IKEA's clever marketing-scheme maze had backfired. I was trapped in an audio labyrinth of predictable chords and cheesy lyrics, and all I wanted to do was get out of the building.

At last, I paid for the few items I'd picked up during my jaunt through the store. Choosing to honor the environmental campaign that discouraged using plastic bags, I stuffed a frying pan into my bookbag and looked for the nearest exit. The ballad was still piercing my brain as the PA system piped the same music into the entryway, so I stopped to speak with the only unengaged employee I could find: the welcome girl.

"Welcome to IKEA," she said, smiling and extending a shopping bag toward me.

Shaking my head, I told her I'd finished shopping. Then I whimpered, pointing to the ceiling, "But I want you to know, the same song has been playing over and over and over and over. I do not like this!"

Still smiling cheerfully, the welcome girl responded, "I don't know."

Unsure of her meaning, I quickly calculated the cost to my dignity if I continued this conversation and lodged an official complaint. No doubt it would require theatrical charades and dramatic facial expressions. Did I really want to get into this discussion in the entryway of IKEA while I was already borderline crazy?

"Never mind, no problem," I said in Cantonese as I smiled and walked away.

But the tune still rang in my ears. "Never let me go… We'll be together forever…"

CHAPTER 22

A POLYGLOT AND OPPOSITES

One of the most striking characteristics of Hong Kong is the paradox of East and West. Sometimes referred to as the "New York City of the East," Hong Kong is just that—a burgeoning metropolis of Western dynamics and culture planted on the soil of Chinese antiquity and tradition. The most obvious source of this attribute is history itself. Under British rule, Hong Kong became an outpost of Western civilization, following England's laws, politics, government, and customs. Gradually, the essence of Hong Kong became a culture unto itself, a unique blend of Western thought and lifestyle with an underlying "Chineseness" still very much a part of daily life.

On the street level, East meets West is evident everywhere. A guy dressed in a Spiderman costume is busking on the sidewalk with a group of people singing Canto-pop songs. Busking itself is a British term referring to the act of standing on street corners or in public places, entertaining passersby through dancing, singing, or other performances.

Meanwhile, the local McDonald's serves red bean pies and offers a side of corn with a Big Mac. The amusement park contains all the usual roller coasters while concession stands offer fried squid for a snack. A locally purchased Scrabble game comes with written instructions translated into Japanese, Thai, and Chinese, both traditional and simplified characters. Prince Edward train station is just a few stops away from Lai Chi Kok station.

Down along the harbor, there is a Hollywood-inspired Avenue of Stars with handprints of famous Asian actors and actresses. A well-known Whitney Houston ballad blares through the loudspeaker at a local market where chickens are butchered. Hong Kong is both Western with Chinese characteristics and Chinese with Western characteristics.

***

An amusing example of this blend occurred in a choir rehearsal I attended. I had joined an English-speaking community choral group after living in Hong Kong for a while, and I appreciated the opportunity to meet new people and experience music-making on a weekly basis.

From time to time, different conductors stepped in to lead us in rehearsals and concerts. For a few months, a diminutive, energetic Chinese woman directed us. As a musician, she was so passionate about her work that she bounced around the room, speaking as if loaded with firecrackers and caffeine. She possessed superb English-speaking skills, but when she grew excited or frustrated, her language morphed into rapid Chinglish and Cantonese with lots of frantic arm-waving.

Within the context of rehearsing a specific passage of a musical work, I could usually figure out what she was asking of us, regardless of the language employed. Often, she demonstrated the incorrect vs. correct way of singing a phrase, making it obvious which she wanted. Exclamations such as "ready, go!" and "sing it again" were spoken in Cantonese. Instruction on vocal intonation was given in English. The count-off to begin singing frequently came out in Cantonese: "*Yat. Yih. Saam.*" One, two, three.

Adding a layer of complication to this English/Cantonese mix, we were rehearsing at the time the original German lyrics of Brahms' *Requiem.* This piece was so difficult and frustrating to learn that the performers were soon wishing they too, like Brahms, were deceased. In Chinglish, the conductor trained us in the proper pronunciation of the German text. She got so involved in the articulation of German that she began counting off, "*Eins. Zwei. Drei.*"

I even heard her say in her own unique blend of Chinglish-German, "*Eins. Yih. Saam.*"

Since music itself employs Italian terminology, our director's Chinglish-German would suddenly be interrupted with cries of "*tutti!*" or "from the *allegro* section" or "more *legato*!"

This grew even more complex. I'd been taught the American-English terminology for musical note types: eighth-note, sixteenth-note, quarter-note, etc. In formerly British Hong Kong, however, people prefer *quaver, semiquaver,* and *crotchet.* My translating mind still took several seconds to recall the meaning of the latter words.

Then one week during a short break halfway through the rehearsal, a fellow alto sat down beside me, asking for help understanding a book she was reading: *Wuthering Heights.* Happy to discuss one of my favorite novels, I agreed. She pointed to a sentence in the second chapter, spoken by a character with a heavy accent.

"T' maister's dahn i' t' fowld. Goa rahnd by th' end ut' laith, if yah went tuh spake tull him."[13]

Dialectical dialogue in nineteenth-century Victorian British literature. Perhaps I'm not a monoglot after all.

***

During my first year of living in Hong Kong, a friend took me to visit a local place of worship called Wong Tai Sin Temple, an area open to tourists as well as those practicing Taoism, Buddhism, and Confucianism. It felt odd to be a sightseer complete with sunglasses, camera, and backpack while watching the devout go through rituals of worship all around me.

The sweet, smoky smell of incense burned my throat and irritated my eyes. Through the haze, I could see employees wearing baggy uniforms, rubber gloves up to their elbows, and thick black boots on their feet. With bored expressions, they removed burned incense sticks from the pots of soil around the altars, dipped them in a bucket of murky water, then dropped them into large rubbish bins.

People there for worship paused before an altar, grasping joss sticks in both hands or sometimes waving them over their heads, while still holding their purse or bag on their shoulder. One woman bowed while another uttered words under her breath. A man chatted on a cell phone as he stood near the altar. Some people seemed to be absorbed in this rite while others appeared distracted.

Before coming to Hong Kong, I'd read in a guidebook that this particular temple was a popular destination for those seeking information about their fortunes, whether advice about business,

[13] Brontë, Emily, *Wuthering Heights* (New York: Bantam Books, 1981), 7.

marriage, horse-racing, or other decisions. Indeed, one entire building of the temple grounds was reserved for fortune-telling booths where you could have your palm or forehead read. For an extra HKD$2 (about USD25¢), you could stroll through the beautiful meditation gardens with goldfish ponds and lush greenery. The mosquitoes came free.

This excursion and others in later years were cultural experiences in which I caught a glimpse of the complex relationship between religion and culture. As a city of commerce, the dollar reigns in Hong Kong. Consumerism and capitalism overshadow all else, it seems. Hong Kong is known for being a hub for business and a setting for headquarters of regional factories. Europeans and North Americans routinely enter the city for meetings, contracts, and factory inspections.

Yet religion inundates local culture. Ancestry worship, Taoism, and various forms of Buddhism pervade everyday life. Altars and familial idols occupy prominent spaces in flats. Religious beliefs and customs dictate both daily choices and momentous decisions, including building architecture and propitious dates for the launching of a new enterprise.

A city of opposites in so many ways. There was still much for me to learn about Hong Kong.

CHAPTER 23

NUMBERS AND AIRMAIL

In addition to language, I had to learn other systems that differed from what I knew in the United States. In Hong Kong, the street-level floor is called the ground floor while the first floor is the next level up. I initially found this bewildering.

Most buildings have no fourth floor. Just as many skyscrapers in North America skip the thirteenth floor due to its association with bad luck, so in Hong Kong the fourth floor is omitted. In Cantonese, the word for four sounds like the word for death, so it is associated with bad luck or misfortune. The fourteenth, twenty-fourth, thirty-fourth, forty-fourth stories, and so on are also left out, though floors forty, forty-one, forty-two, etc. are included. When discussing how many stories some of the city's tallest structures contain, I am still unclear how to calculate the total. Do we count according to the highest number listed on the elevator buttons or the number of actual physical floors?

A bilingual sign used to hang in my apartment building stairwell next to the fire extinguisher that read tenth floor in English and ninth floor in Chinese. Which is to say, the same level had two different numbers depending on whether you read the English or

Chinese. If I had to call the fire department in a panic, asking for rescue, perhaps the operator would say, "Certainly, ma'am, we'll send a team to rescue you from the life-threatening flames that are engulfing your building. One question, though. Which system of floor labeling do you adhere to?"

Systems of all kinds exist in Hong Kong, requiring me to adjust. Most of the world, apart from America, follows the metric system. Hong Kong, however, employs a curious mix of three systems: metric, imperial (i.e., the British Empire system of pounds, feet, miles, etc.), and some elements of an ancient Chinese method of measurement. An example of the latter is the catty, a unit of mass equal to about 604 grams, used for weighing food in local markets.

When discussing area of buildings or flats, square feet are typically employed. I hear women mentioning the birth weight of babies in pounds. The guy who cuts my hair always speaks of trimming off inches. Yet all street signs and road markings display metric units.

Speed and distance are measured in kilometers. Cars have metric speedometers. Motorists purchase gas in liters. Beverages in the supermarkets come in liters and milliliters. Western-style grocery stores contain an amalgamation of metric and imperial systems, depending on the item's country of origin. A bag of potatoes from North America weighs two pounds while a package of spuds from Australia weighs one kilo.

Dates are typically written in the format *dd/mm/yyyy*, although Chinese language items sometimes employ *yyyy/mm/dd*. When checking the expiration date of food, one has to first verify the product's source. Or just take a bite and hope for the best.

To summon ambulance or police, the number to call is 999. I fear that if I ever encounter an emergency, I'll default to 911, then panic trying to recall the correct number of the Hong Kong system. Is it 991? 111? 919?

In summary, my new life in Hong Kong contained a discombobulated mix of many systems, and I found myself frequently using the wrong one... and wishing I'd paid more attention in grade-school math classes.

***

Hong Kong is one of the leading financial capitals on the globe, a city known for its technology and industry. But a stop into a Hong Kong post office makes me feel I've traveled back a hundred years. I see aging white concrete walls, dark-brown molding, glass-windowed counters, green lettering and design. Some post offices have low ceilings, dim lighting, dingy windows, and a lazy ceiling fan rotating above. A wooden counter holds pens attached to chains and a wet sponge for moistening envelopes and stamps.

Employees use ordinary calculators to figure postage amounts, then open a cardboard book held together with rubber bands and Scotch tape. Each section of the book holds various denominations of perforated stamps. The postal worker tears them out one by one until the correct postage is collected in a neat pile for the customer to affix on their parcel.

Cashiers complete further calculations by hand, scribbling on scraps of paper or the package itself. The pencil came from a holder constructed of a cut-off paper towel roll. No self-adhesive stamps or digital scales. No computerized printing of postage. Credit cards are not accepted, cash in small denominations only.

However, the postal workers themselves must be highly educated and intelligent since Hong Kong mail can be confusing. Addresses of local flats or businesses are complex in that they include street names, building names, tower numbers or letters, building numbers or letters, floor numbers, flat numbers or letters, etc. Additionally, an address or name can be penned in any of the three written languages used in the territory: traditional Chinese characters, simplified characters, or English.

In recent years, some local post offices have begun installing computers, scales, and technology that can produce a self-adhesive sticker notating the total postage paid, thus eliminating the need for multiple stamps for a single package. Nevertheless, many of my post office experiences remain exasperating and time-consuming, leaving me wondering why the digital age hasn't reached the postal department.

On one such warm afternoon, I arrived at a post office in Kowloon. This was a single narrow, dim room with numbered windows and counters along one wall. Each window contained a sign to help the customer determine where to go: packages, packages and small matter, large packages, letters, pay-thru-post, and philately (stamp collecting or purchasing). I had two items to mail—a small box and one large envelope. Deciding I needed to approach the counter labeled "small packages," I waited my turn in the queue.

When I pushed my items through the opening in the glass, the employee inquired, "By air or ground?"

"By air," I replied.

"Do you need insurance or registration?"

"No."

The man then informed me I was at the wrong counter. The oversized envelope should be mailed from the "letters" counter because it was not, in fact, a package. Then he placed my small box on the scale and stated that the price would be HKD$151 if I mailed it from one counter and HKD$149 from another counter.

"Which counter is the cheaper one?" I asked him.

"Air or ground?" he asked again.

"Air," I responded.

"Ground is cheaper. But air is a different price. It's $151 or $149, depending on how you mail it."

"Okay, but which way is cheaper?" I repeated.

"Ground is cheaper than air."

I understood *that*. What I wasn't grasping was how the same package sent by air could cost more or less depending on which counter it was sent out from. *Please just tell me which counter offers the cheaper price!*

It did occur to me that the difference equaled about USD25¢—hardly worth the trouble. The poor gentleman behind the glass made a valiant effort to help me, but I left his window still confused with two un-mailed items in hand. Why was this so difficult?

After another wait in line, I approached counter number one, thinking I could at least mail the large envelope. The postal employee there—perhaps sensing I was an ignorant foreigner—accepted both of my items, weighed them, scribbled the postage amount on each package, and handed me a pile of stamps. I had to lick and stick individual stamps, six to ten per item. The thought of germs transferring from the stamps to my tongue was disturbing, but so was the dirty, damp sponge provided for this purpose, which had been sitting out in the heat all day. The international customs form likewise required moisture, though at least the airmail labels were adhesive stickers.

Upon finishing my licking and sticking, I located yet another counter where the packages had to be re-checked by another employee and dropped into the appropriate bin. I was weary and worn, but my small box and large envelope were on their way—hopefully by air—to their respective destinations.

Finally exiting the building, I hoped my mother would enjoy her birthday gift. Next year maybe I'd shop online with free delivery.

CHAPTER 24

BIRDS AND CREMATORIUMS

"Wild birds are not pets," Jackie Chan advised a class of school children in a public service announcement (PSA) I saw on television shortly after moving to Hong Kong. In the midst of an avian flu scare, the government was urging citizens to refrain from handling birds and their feces.

"Of course, paper cranes are excluded," Chan laughed as he picked up an origami creation. The children responded with giggles.

Hong Kong is a city that revels in PSAs and advertisements aimed at the general community. How to treat one another. Health reminders. Statements of caution. Notices about laws and regulations. Care for the environment and more.

Runner-up on my list of favorite PSAs featured Jackie Chan and pal Arnold Schwarzenegger on hot-rod motorcycles racing down the highway as they exclaimed, "Piracy is a crime. When you make illegal copies of movies, we all lose." They popped a wheelie and zoomed off into the sunset.

One year during the Olympics, I spent a ridiculous amount of time watching the Games on local television. I'd already noticed that Hong Kong advertising—whether printed or televised—seemed designed to appeal to a younger audience. North American commercials entertain with cinematic filmmaking and sophisticated wit, albeit through spending outrageous amounts of money. Hong Kong commercials more typically employ a cartoonish figure or dancing actor singing a song about the product.

Yet, what shocked me while observing these local commercials was the overwhelmingly disproportionate number of PSAs on Hong Kong television. Furthermore, the range of topics addressed in these ads was wide and varied. In two weeks of Olympics-watching—with dutiful note taking—here is a small sampling of what I saw:

- Food safety: Be careful of food temperatures. Do not leave food sitting out, as it may spoil.
- Be prepared before taking part in water activities. Check the weather forecast, drink plenty of water, and wear safety gear.
- We must take proper care of trees so we can live in harmony with the trees.
- Adopt reasonable employment terms and treat employees properly.
- No matter how busy you are, try to exercise every day.
- In case of fire, leave your flat and take with you a mobile phone (to call for help), a towel (to cover your nose and mouth), and your door keys (so you can return afterwards).
- Mutual respect, communication, and understanding lead to social harmony.

- There is a new lift and elevator ordinance which will help with strengthening regulatory control and enhancing public safety.
- Sleep and wake early, eat vegetables and drink water, start your exercise journey, don't worry and be happy, make this a healthier city.
- Join hands to maintain the cleanliness of public swimming pools.
- If trapped in a lift, stand still, crouch down, sit down, and stay calm.
- Invest carefully. Signing means responsibility.
- Be cautious when purchasing columbarium niches [a place to store ashes].

These kinds of announcements are certainly effective. To this day when I see bird droppings, I think of Jackie Chan. I then remember his admonishment that we should not consider wild birds as pets. Nor touch their droppings.

***

One Friday evening, I made my way to a street lined with funeral parlors to attend a Christian memorial service. The large, imposing buildings had dull gray exteriors. Hole-in-the-wall shops clustered along the edges of the neighborhood streets, each selling fresh flowers, caskets, or the paper effigies used in these settings. The remains of mourning littered the curbs and sidewalks: crushed flower petals, dried leaves, a bit of ribbon or paper, discarded tissue, and incense scraps. Groups of male employees huddled in the cold on the steps of the building, smoking and stretching their legs.

Upon entering the appointed building, I immediately noticed the din of talkative crowds, jarring music, and the smoky haze of burning incense. There was a lobby with one aging elevator and several floors of small rooms reserved for particular families. The dividing lines among religions were clearly visible. Christian mourners dressed in solid black clothing while Taoists or Buddhists were clothed in white from head to toe. Sprinkled in were a few shaven Buddhist monks wearing habits of burgundy or saffron.

At the doorway of each room was a reception table. Guests would sign their name in a book, then receive a small white packet. Its contents included a piece of fruit candy, a coin, and one tissue. I later learned that the candy represents the sweetness of life that mingles with the sadness. Tradition dictates that this should be eaten immediately. The coin is symbolic of ensuring the mourners return home safely, and the tissue is for tears. By custom, the recipients should throw away the white envelope, a remnant of sadness.

Guests brought a separate white packet, which contained a bit of cash to help the family with the funeral expenses. In Hong Kong, even numbers represent happiness, which is unsuitable for a time of grief, so money was given in odd amounts.

Inside the rectangular room, tall flower arrangements lined the walls, each labeled with prominent black-and-white signs indicating who had given the bouquet. An altar of sorts sat at the front of the room, on which was situated a large photo of the deceased surrounded by flowers and candles. The relatives were seated on the left. Walking forward, guests bowed three times toward the altar and once to the family. It hadn't occurred to me to ask my Hong Kong friends about funeral customs beforehand, so I blindly followed what other people were doing, hoping I wouldn't offend anyone.

Family members and friends chatted together despite regular interruptions from the presiding announcer, who counted to three into a microphone each time a guest arrived to bow and pay respect. Din from the next-door room disrupted much of the conversation. For Taoist funerals, it is customary for priests to play loud music on drums, cymbals, flutes, and other instruments in addition to chanting. I was uncertain of the exact significance of these elements, but the cacophony felt unsettling.

As I departed after the funeral service, I passed by hallways lined with massive paper or cardboard structures. A child-sized mansion. A miniature luxury car. A stack of fake cash. A bridge. A cluster of paper dolls. I was told these items were symbolic of wealth and could be purchased and burned for the deceased to enjoy in the afterlife. In any other setting—a shopping mall or amusement park, for example—they would have been interesting to inspect and photograph, but here they seemed a bit sad.

The following morning, I arrived at a crematorium building for the next portion of the funeral proceedings. The crematorium complex included small chapel-like rooms and rows of slots in which ashes resided. Entering one of the rooms, I found a seat on a well-worn wooden bench. The ceiling was high, the doors open, and a crisp breeze made its way through the enclosure. I detected a faint whiff of smoke and incense, but the airy room kept the circulation flowing pleasantly.

After a few words, a Bible reading, and a prayer, the immediate family stepped forward. The casket had been resting on a short conveyor belt at the front of the room. This was a typical metal and rubber piece of equipment such as would be found in an airport terminal. In a moment of solemnity and grief, the family members pressed a large green button that set the conveyor belt into motion.

Guests stood and watched as the casket slowly glided through a low doorway. The doors closed, and the casket was gone.

To me, the pressing of the button was a curious inclusion in the service. It brought a feeling of closure. Yet by watching, I felt I was intruding on a personal moment that should have been reserved for the family alone. Nevertheless, a pragmatic way to close the funeral rite.

Thereafter, family members and guests headed to a nearby restaurant where everyone would enjoy a feast. Good food is a comfort in all cultures.

CHAPTER 25

NAPKINS AND DIM SUM

One unique aspect of living as an expat abroad is how we share our belongings with one another. More specifically, what we share. When one American couple left Hong Kong and moved back to the States, they bequeathed to me a bag full of party napkins. There were American flag napkins, Thanksgiving-themed napkins, baby shower napkins, etc. These used to be difficult to find in Hong Kong, so they were considered valuable. Later I found out these very napkins had passed through several hands over the years. Apparently, they were too priceless to actually use.

Other curious items such as board games, spices, organic flour, candles, cake pans, muffin papers, ice trays, and balloons have all come into my possession from other foreigners. One woman bestowed upon me a high-quality piece of Tupperware before leaving the city. Turning over the container, I saw surnames of two other American families written in permanent marker and crossed out. I drew a line through my friend's name and added mine below, ensuring it would always be returned to me if borrowed.

When people move within the United States, they might leave a favorite potted plant or stack of books to a friend, but not a jar of pumpkin pie spice or a package of Super Bowl napkins. What is valuable and priceless changes depending on location and availability. Beauty is in the eye of the beholder, and one person's trash is another person's treasure.

* * *

Gathering with other foreigners in Hong Kong is always a fascinating experience. In my job working for a church, I am periodically invited to join a lunch for international exchange students at a local university. I go to introduce our church and be a "face of the local community" by welcoming these newly arrived young people to the city.

At one such occasion on a hot August afternoon, I arrived at the appointed restaurant with hundreds of students, professors, and community members. I sat down at my assigned table with seven students from seven different countries: Czech Republic, France, Hong Kong (a local student assisting with the welcome activities), Germany, Mainland China, Denmark, and the Netherlands.

I began with the usual get-to-know-you questions. "What's your name? Where are you from? What are you studying? When did you arrive in Hong Kong?"

Our conversations then diverged into many directions. In an effort to engage the Czech girl sitting next to me, I rambled aimlessly about this local university they'd be attending.

"It's about fifty years old, which is actually quite young. The university I attended in the US is over a hundred and fifty years old," I thoughtlessly bragged.

She politely responded, "My school was founded in the fourteenth century."

Huh.

Our table of mismatched strangers continued chatting. One asked, "Are there any good French restaurants in Hong Kong?"

I had no idea. The local Hong Kong student didn't know either.

"If we travel in China while we're here, where should we go?" several students asked.

I suggested two highly recommended locations, both popular among tourists. No, I hadn't been to either place, I admitted. Unfortunately, there'd be no long holiday breaks during the fall semester—unlike the spring semester, which contained both Chinese New Year and Easter breaks, providing more time for students to travel.

"Most international students here for the fall semester skip out on classes for a few days or a week so they can go sight-seeing in a nearby country," I offered. Then I bit my tongue. What kind of advice was I—"a face of the local community"—giving by encouraging these neophytes to play hooky?

I tried to be the hospitable host for my half of the table, refilling teacups and placing dim sum items into bowls. I ended up spilling boiling water all over the tablecloth.

"At least I didn't drop a spring roll into my cup," I chuckled. The students smiled kindly.

"Is there any difference between Catholics and Baptists?" piped up the French student.

"Well, a few," I responded. The restaurant was too loud for any serious theological discussion, but I shouted out a quick run-down of the basics.

The conversational noise increased as the meal began to wrap up. Regrettably, the food we'd been served was a poor excuse for the delicacies of traditional dim sum and Cantonese fare.

"Don't judge Hong Kong cuisine by this sad institutional-quality food," I told my guests.

"It's the best we've had so far," the students politely responded.

Like kindergarteners, the two hundred-plus undergrads were dismissed for their next activity in order of table number. We stood, closed with the niceties expected after such an occasion, and moved in different directions.

This international lunch was a snapshot of a typical Hong Kong experience for me. Thrown into a socially awkward situation with people from all walks of life and regions of the globe. Completely different personalities and worldviews. Discussing multiple topics from food, travel, cultures and language, to religion, music, and history. Being asked curious questions about the United States. Occasionally being the expert on Hong Kong (when interacting with a newcomer), but usually being the foreign idiot (when chatting with everyone else).

These are the reasons I love Hong Kong. You never know who you'll encounter or what you'll learn from another expat or local. The "internationalness," I like to call it. Never a dull moment. Always having to be on your toes. Not sure what kinds of people will walk into your life tomorrow.

Hong Kong. Asia's World City.

CHAPTER 26

GECKOS AND PEACOCKS

During the early years of living in my Hong Kong flat, I engaged in regular battle with a gecko. He hibernated for weeks and months at a time, then would make a sudden appearance in my kitchen, usually when I had guests over for dinner. The first time this occurred, I thought it was a fluke. After the second and third time, I declared war on the ill-mannered creature.

After catching—and safely releasing outdoors—several such geckos, I determined the cracks and crevices in my kitchen were not the bachelor pad of a single Lone Ranger reptile, but rather an Ancestral Home wherein offspring were brought into this world in litters and herds. These young were reared and taught the lifestyle habits of their parental units. Namely, frighten the human homeowner to the extent that she surrenders the use of the kitchen, thereby enlarging the gecko Ancestral Home.

This was not without precedent. I awoke one morning to a rustling noise underneath my bed. Investigating, I discovered that a large, unidentifiable flying insect had somehow wheedled its way into my flat. Its body was at least an inch long with a correspondingly wide wingspan. After chasing this fiend around the bedroom for a bit, I cornered it behind an unmovable armoire. There it huddled, refusing to be coaxed out.

My solution, born in desperation, was to gather up a few necessities, firmly close the bedroom door, seal the doorframe with towels, and sleep on the sofa the following night. It took about twenty-four hours, but eventually the flying intruder expired. Scooping it up, I dumped it in the trash and boldly reclaimed full command of my bedroom.

Perhaps that Flying One—before its passing—conveyed my tactics to the gecko family, who decided to follow the same approach in hopes I would cede my kitchen to the reptilian community.

Au contraire.

After seeking advice from a few locals, I accepted from one helpful Hong Konger a small metal can of glue that would supposedly trap a gecko. This was by no means a new purchase. The can was rusted, paint peeling off the sides, precluding the possibility of reading any instructions. With determination, I marched into my kitchen that evening, pried the lid off the ancient tin, then gasped as a strong, foul odor hit me full in the face. If it wouldn't ensnare the lizards, it would at least frighten off any other would-be intruders, including humans.

There was no doubt about this glue being powerful enough to entrap a six-inch long, four-legged creature. Thicker than molasses, the glob of dark-brown adhesive didn't come easily out of the can, no matter how much I tried to pour and shake. Grabbing a knife, I attempted to scrape some goop onto a piece of cardboard I'd arranged on the counter for this purpose. I quickly found myself tangled up in a mess of sticky paste—cardboard, knife, fingers, and glue canister all cemented together. It took some time and most of a bottle of nail polish remover to get things sorted out and unstuck.

Looking around for suitable lizard bait, I chose dollops of spaghetti. The stench of the glue so overwhelmed my entire flat a few morsels of rotten food couldn't make it any worse. If the gecko couldn't smell my offering, I hoped the tantalizing sight of marinara sauce and pasta would lure him to his adhesive demise.

The next morning, I ran eagerly to the kitchen to view my catch.

Nothing.

The smell of the paste had so permeated my home that in the end I decided I actually preferred geckos. Perhaps the glue had served its purpose after all.

***

In the weeks and months that followed, lizard sightings grew so few and far between that I began to grow lax. I walked into the kitchen while simultaneously turning on the light rather than flipping on the light and banging on the door first as a warning to any unsuspecting critters. I brazenly entered the room in the dark without fear or trepidation. Many times. In fact, I completely forgot about my flatmates and their Ancestral Home.

Until…

It was evening. The kitchen had been dark for some time when I stepped into the room in search of a late-night snack. I flipped on the light and found myself staring into the bulging eyes of an alarmed, pinkish-white fellow. He cocked his head to one side. I froze. He skittered off to the corner. I scrounged for a bowl in which to trap him. He took refuge behind a flour canister. I rattled the stovetop burners to scare him out of hiding. He ran into a microscopic gap between the wall and cabinet. I threw up my hands in defeat. Suddenly, that bedtime bowl of cereal didn't sound as tempting.

Once again filled with willpower and fortitude, I gritted my teeth and determined to resolve the issue once and for all. Geckos inhabit most of Southeast Asia because they prefer warm tropical climates, but I was the one paying the utility bills in this flat.

I turned to the source of knowledge and Googled how to get rid of lizards in the home. Answers from all corners of the globe immediately filled my screen. Get a cat. Keep your home clean. Don't leave food out on the counter. Let the geckos live—they eat insects. Spray a complicated watery solution of liquid plant food on the walls. Seal up all cracks and crevices outside your home. Cut the grass and remove shrubbery from underneath the windows. Keep the home cool and dry.

None of these options sounded viable for my situation. I didn't want an indoor feline. I was already a persnickety housekeeper. If I used any more anti-bacterial, bleach-based cleaning products in my home, I might exterminate myself. My kitchen cupboards had been installed on top of previous structures when the kitchen was refurbished, so sealing up the crevices would be an impossible feat (and was probably the reason my flat was chosen as the site for the Gecko Ancestral Home). Obviously, I had no shrubbery issue around my high-rise home. And because I lived in a subtropical climate, I would never be able to maintain cool, dry conditions inside.

Setting out mothballs was another frequently suggested solution, though the very thought of replacing that glue stench with the sickly-sweet pungency of camphor kept me clicking in search of a less malodorous remedy. Other netizens offered the idea of placing empty eggshells around the areas where geckos dwelled. Exactly how eggshells would repel such creatures was never explained. One blogger wrote that she'd observed a haughty lizard perched atop such an eggshell, leading her to conclude the method wasn't effective. Forget that option.

Oddly, more than one website recommended laying peacock feathers near the gecko's residence. An internet link below this suggestion was labeled, "How to catch a peacock." Not owning a large wire cage for such a bird was just one of many deterrents preventing me from following this recommendation. My goal was the removal of lizards and all other living creatures from my home. No need to catch a bear to catch a dog to catch a cat to catch a peacock to catch the gecko—who wasn't assisting me in catching unwelcome flying insects anyway.

My confusion grew and my resolve weakened until, with a mouse-click, I closed the browser and gave up the battle. After all, it was just one or two geckos.

Unfortunately, one of the last things I read in my internet search was that a gecko's lifespan could be as long as five years. I wondered just how many extended family members lived in the Ancestral Home hidden away in my kitchen walls.

CHAPTER 27

VISAS AND STICKERS

I came to Hong Kong on a work visa, which I had to renew periodically. One day while sorting old paperwork, I discovered that my visa would expire in less than a month, an issue compounded by the fact that I planned to travel in three weeks. Knowing the typical bureaucracy for any kind of application procedure, I immediately embarked on a search for the necessary documents.

I'd dealt with this issue before. But I could never remember what paperwork was necessary, which floor of the Hong Kong Immigration Tower to go to, or what forms to fill out. In these situations, I inevitably ended up at the wrong counter without a particular document and would be sent away in shame. This time, I searched the appropriate website for clues as to what I should bring. I didn't bother to print and fill out a form in advance as I couldn't even figure out what category of visa applicant applied to me.

The next morning, I awoke two hours early, dreading the day's task. Choosing a large backpack, I set out to gather everything I might possibly need. Papers. Signed letters with the appropriate "chops" (a stamp or seal used across Asia by government agencies and businesses, like a corporate signature). Many documents.

Multiple photocopies of my passport and ID card. Might they want my United Airlines frequent flier card too?

Assuming I'd be spending exorbitant amounts of time waiting in lines, I filled up a water bottle and grabbed some snacks. I added a fully-charged iPod and cell phone. A pack of gum. One newspaper and a seven-hundred-page book. I should be okay for a day or two.

Since I don't typically use public transportation before 8 a.m., the morning rush-hour crowd caught me by surprise. My trip across the city took nearly an hour, and the crush of humanity continued throughout the walk from the train station to the Immigration Tower. The building had armed guards in the lobby and an intimidating directory covering an entire wall from floor to ceiling. Not certain of my destination, I bypassed the lift and stepped onto the escalators, planning to study the signs on each floor as I went up.

I finally found a section with counters labeled "forms" and "enquiries." Surprisingly, there were no lines at either counter, so I wound my way through an empty maze of ropes, like at an airport security gate, and approached the window. A pleasant gentleman sat surrounded by stacks of papers that piled up higher than his head. When I explained my situation, he immediately rifled through a sheaf of documents and handed me a blank form.

I was equally amazed to locate an empty area at a row of desks which people like me could use to complete paperwork. With plenty of space, I dumped my bag and began filling in the blanks on the form—of course writing in block letters using blue or black ink. Papers in hand, I continued up the escalators until I found the appropriate floor for my visa application.

There I joined the queue at a counter labeled "those without appointments." The signage made me feel inadequate as if I'd failed in my responsibilities, but I was pleased when the line moved quickly. A woman studied my form, and then took my passport and printed out a receipt with a number: B26. Very efficient. On my previous visits, they'd just scribbled a number in marker on a bit of scratch paper.

I sighed as I examined the rows of chairs in the waiting area and located a place to settle. I took my time as I removed my coat, slathered my hands with anti-bacteria gel, and put away the ream of unnecessary documents I'd toted along. Glancing up at the wall in front of me, I saw a television screen that hadn't been there on my last visit. It displayed the numbers visually as clerks called out the numbers audibly.

My usual task at this point was to practice my numbers in Cantonese, hoping I'd recognize mine when it was called rather than wait for the receptionist to repeat it in exasperated English. But what was this? According to the television screen, they were currently on number B22. I was fourth in line. How had this miraculous turn of events come about?

While I was relishing my good fortune, a voice announced my number. Gathering my belongings, I went up to the counter. With a cheerful smile, the woman behind the glass asked me a few questions and studied my paperwork. I was prepared to plead my case: that I would be traveling out of the city soon and needed to rush the visa application through.

But before I could even embark on my preplanned speech, the woman graciously agreed to look into it. "Please find a seat and wait for me to call you again."

Okay, this is when the wait begins, I told myself dully. I should have known it's a two-part process.

Planting myself in a chair, I located my newspaper. Civil unrest in Libya. After scrutinizing the grainy front-page photo, I began reading the article. Suddenly, I heard my name over the loud-speaker. Not B26. My name.

Frazzled, I once again gathered my gear and located the counter to which I'd been summoned. The same kind woman returned my passport, then handed me a slip of paper listing the date when I could return and collect my visa—five days before my upcoming trip. She smiled, thanked me, and turned away.

With some confusion, I asked, "So what do I do next?"

"Nothing."

"You mean I'm finished? I can leave now?"

She nodded.

But I hadn't even read the front page of the newspaper. I never got to practice my Cantonese numbers. I was supposed to have an eventful ordeal that included committing embarrassing language blunders, filling out the wrong forms, and waiting in long queues like a featherbrained foreigner. What about the banana located at the bottom of my backpack? The seven hundred pages of my book? The crossword puzzle in the newspaper?

No matter. At this early morning hour, the shopping center I'd planned to visit after my visa excursion was not yet open. So there would be some waiting after all.

* * *

I love getting mail. Real mail. Those bits of tangible paper in crisp envelopes covered in picturesque stamps, postmarks, and scrawling script. Sometimes there's even a cute little airplane sticker on the outside, indicating airmail.

The lobby of my building holds rows of mailboxes beside the elevator. My mailbox consists of a small metal container with a slit into which the postman can stuff envelopes and thin packets. Anything larger requires me to take a special trip to the post office twenty minutes down the road to retrieve the item. Once, I received a parcel about the size of a VHS tape. Rather than making me journey to the post office, the mailman kindly and artfully hung the package from the outside of my mailbox using a complicated system of twine and rubber bands.

Occasionally, I receive a nice letter or postcard from a friend, or a magazine or bill. Mostly, though, my mailbox contains junk mail. Sometimes it's a leaflet with pictures from a real estate agency trying to summon new business. Other times it will be an ad for a local tutoring center or an advertisement for swimming or piano lessons. I may find a public service announcement offering tips on taking care of household appliances or reminding me to keep an eye on the condition of my windowpanes (so the frame doesn't fall out and wound an innocent bystander).

I frequently receive a colorful ad from a nearby supermarket. Though no products are listed in English, I usually study the pictures to ascertain what items are on sale. Pizza Hut once sent me a flyer introducing a new offering: Surf Clam and Crab Stick Sesame Stuffed Crust Pizza (try saying that three times in a row). A tri-fold brochure from KFC informs me that I can purchase wasabi hot wings or egg tarts with my chicken combo.

One afternoon as I was waiting in line at the post office to mail a few letters, I noticed a billboard announcing: "No Circular Mail." I first sorted out what "circular mail" meant. The phrase had nothing to do with the shape of a circle but referred to impersonal mail-outs. To opt out from receiving unaddressed mail or bulk advertisements, I just needed to place a green oval sticker on the outside of my mailbox, and—ta-da!—no more junk mail. Moreover, the sticker was free and sitting right there on the post office counter.

So I took one.

I felt quite proud as I placed the sticker on the upper right-hand corner of my mailbox. I was protecting the environment by cutting down on unnecessary paper. And the green oval—referred to as the "Sticker Scheme"—worked. For six days in a row, I found my box completely empty.

No more supermarket ads with pictures of strange meat or indistinguishable cleaning products. No more cartoon characters reminding me to call the gas company if I smelled something suspect or to watch for break-ins if scaffolding covered my building. Not one brochure with colorful photographs of a new apartment building with seven-hundred-square-foot flats for rent. No more flyers with misspelled words offering to tutor my child in English.

I congratulated myself for doing my part as a good citizen. But in truth, my life grew just a little more boring now that one of my major forms of entertainment had vanished.

CHAPTER 28

ABCS AND WORMS

In the fall of my second or third year in Hong Kong, a large organization from the States held a conference at a local coliseum. After the program was over, I joined a group of volunteers to help disassemble the equipment and reset the furniture we'd moved. People from various groups in Hong Kong as well as from the United States came to assist, many of whom were ABCs, or American-born Chinese. This is a particularly confusing demographic as ABCs look Chinese but are American through and through. They often speak little or no Cantonese or Mandarin.

At one point, several university students had gathered a stack of boxes that needed to be placed in a truck out in the parking lot. One Chinese-looking guy yelled in English to the driver, "Where's your truck? We need to load this stuff."

The driver looked at him blankly, appearing not to understand the English question. The Chinese guy turned to another Asian-looking volunteer standing nearby. "Can you translate? Ask him where his truck is."

"Dude!" the second guy responded with a laugh. "I'm Korean!"

"Doesn't anyone around here speak Chinese?" the first guy asked in exasperation.

As fascinated as I was with this conversation, in the absence of a true expert I decided to help out. Using the limited Cantonese I knew—about four words that would actually be useful in this context—I asked the driver the location of his truck.

"On the ground floor," he answered in English.

Well.

It took an unnecessarily long time to get those boxes loaded, but I enjoyed this clash of cultures. Non-Cantonese-speaking Chinese, Koreans who are mistaken for Chinese, Hong Kong people who speak some English but not enough to communicate in this context, and a dumb *gweilo*[14] who mistakenly thinks she can help translate in this insane conversation.

***

Following this event, two other expat friends and I climbed into a waiting taxi a little after midnight. Once we'd verified that the taxi driver was willing to make a cross-harbor trip from Hong Kong-side to Kowloon-side, one friend rattled off our addresses in Cantonese and we settled back in our seats. Many Hong Kong taxi drivers appear sullen and quiet, but this one was especially chatty and eager to converse in English.

"Your Cantonese very good," he complimented the friend who'd given directions. "How long you live in Hong Kong?"

---

[14] The Cantonese term *gweilo* literally translates "ghost man" or "foreign devil," and properly refers to a Caucasian man, but is often used slangily (though incorrectly) to refer to any Westerner, male or female. The correct term for a foreign female is *gweipo*.

“Three years,” my friend replied.

“How do you like Hong Kong?” he asked. This was a typical question, I’d discovered. Hong Kongers appear eager for foreigners to compliment their city.

“We like it very much,” we chorused.

“Where are you from?” the taxi driver asked us.

“The United States,” two of us said.

“Where in America do you live?”

We named our respective home states.

“I’ve been to Los Angeles before,” he proudly proclaimed. A few moments later, he added, “Hong Kong people work very hard. Do you agree?”

“Yes,” we agreed.

“I work very hard. I work many, many hours driving taxi. You call me any time, even in the night, and I will take you where you need to go.”

“Thank you,” we replied.

As we neared our destination, he announced, “I give you good price. A good price for an old friend. If you need to go to airport, I give you good price. Twenty-percent discount. You call me. I come get you and take you to the airport.”

“We will remember,” we promised.

Before we exited the taxi, the driver pulled out a “business card,” which was actually his name and phone number hastily scrawled across the back of an old lottery ticket. I suppose he hoped to make money one way or another, whether through hard work or hitting the jackpot.

"You call me. I am Joe. I will give you good price. Anytime."

***

It was lunchtime, and I had joined a group of friends at a newly-opened Texas barbecue restaurant in the New Territories called Anthony's Ranch. The restaurant advertised barbecue, steaks, ribs, and "Wild West Dining." Their flyer described the location as "the barn next to the [Buddhist] temple."

Though nestled among local shops and eateries, the outside of this restaurant consisted of a red barn façade complete with a life-sized wooden cowboy on one side of the door and a cigar store wooden Native American on the other. Apart from these American relics, one would be hard-pressed to identify it as a barbecue-eating establishment since it lacked proper signage.

"Once we get the necessary permits, we're going to hang up a large Texas flag and an American flag along with a big cow," our host, who turned out to be Anthony himself, informed us.

The menu was written in proper English apart from the "southernisms" added for artistic touch, such as: "Ya'll come and git it, ya hear?" Each dish was uniquely named in Texas lingo: "Chili (not hot, add cheese if y'all want)." Made me feel right at home.

I enjoyed what was probably the best barbecue brisket sandwich I'd eaten in years. The American beef was cooked to perfection. Anthony offered us a ten-minute lecture on the finest way to cook beef. Applewood or other fruit tree wood, not hickory or mesquite, he argued. He used apple, pear, maple, and oak wood for his smoking process. His beef came from a ranch in California.

Turned out this Yankee was from Connecticut operating a Texas-style barbecue place in Hong Kong selling West Coast meat. Anthony went on to explain that the wood chips used for smoking the beef came from China, so "we have to make do with what we can get." Also, food had to be prepared with the local clientele in mind, which meant non-spicy, non-peppery, with little flavor. (Unlike Sichuan and some other Mainland China cuisines, Cantonese food is typically mild as Hong Kong chefs aspire to preserve the ingredients' natural flavors.)

The decor of this dive was unique. On one side, a Confederate flag hung from the ceiling. Another wall was bedecked with black-and-white photograph reprints of the Old West. When I entered the restaurant, the first thing that caught my attention was a huge snake head with jaws open and fangs protruding. The thing was obviously rubber and larger than a human head.

"My grandfather killed that sucker," Anthony claimed, sounding like a typical Texas braggart.

Various metal stars, ropes, antique pistols, and other paraphernalia took up the remainder of the wall space. Waiters, all of them local Hong Kongers, wore cowboy hats. The bar, consisting of two stools and a few small tables, was set apart by a three-foot-high wooden rail complete with a saloon-style swinging door. The entire establishment looked like it would hold no more than twenty people.

When I looked around for the restroom, I was told, "Go out the back door."

Exiting the rear door, I found myself literally outside. I stood in an alley cordoned off by sheet-metal walls surrounded by stacks of stored items draped in red and blue striped tarps. It was raining lightly. I'm definitely still in Hong Kong, I thought.

Nonetheless, the food was delicious, the atmosphere charming, the service great, the owner amusing—if a bit overzealous about cooking beef. There were even free drink refills, and ice was added to the water glasses without my begging. My final comment on the whole affair: "Golly, that 'us sum goooood food!"

***

A few months later, I partook in another protein-laden meal, though this form of protein was unintentional. I was eating lunch with colleagues at a clubhouse-type restaurant, where we ordered various Western dishes from the menu. I chose a hamburger. When it arrived, I removed some excess lettuce and tomatoes and placed them on another plate.

I'd eaten half my hamburger and was deep in conversation when I glanced down and spied a small—but very much alive—worm crawling across the extra lettuce I'd discarded. Breaking off mid-sentence, I put down my burger and watched as this minuscule worm raised its upper half. He performed a mid-air dance, as if mocking me, then continued traversing the vegetables.

I didn't finish my hamburger. Nor did we have to pay for it. And I gladly accepted as compensation a free refill on iced tea. With extra ice.

CHAPTER 29

LUGGAGE AND PILGRIMS

It didn't take me long to discover that Hong Kongers were fanatic about freebies and special "buy-one-get-one" deals. One day, I hunted for a new suitcase at a shopping center where few employees spoke English. With a wide selection of products to browse and low prices on cheaply made items, the shop proved to be a wise choice. No need to spend lots of money on luggage when the airlines would beat it up anyway.

Making my decision, I indicated I was ready to purchase a particular suitcase. The saleswoman then pointed to another small bag on a nearby shelf. Thinking she wanted me to buy it, I politely declined. After she made several further attempts to draw my attention to it, I deduced that I could buy it along with my main purchase for just a few dollars more. I was not interested in the bag, so I continued shaking my head.

The saleswoman then pointed to a photo of a large bag of rice, implying that I could take it instead of the handbag. More head shaking and "don't want, don't need" comments from me in Cantonese resulted in an English-speaking saleswoman being summoned. Her employee lanyard read "Off Duty," but in a mixture of English, Cantonese, and hand gestures, she patiently explained that the bag of rice was a free gift, and it would be silly of me to decline such an offer. No matter that I was a single woman who might take years to consume a five-kilo bag of rice. Or that I was tired and didn't feel like schlepping it home.

The first saleswoman gave fifteen minutes of her time to help me check out, then find the escalator and journey to another floor to locate the customer service counter and retrieve my free gift. My excitement about the new lightweight piece of luggage was severely dampened when I had to haul it home filled with rice.

What struck me as odd about these kinds of situations was not the free gift concept itself. After all, "buy one, get one free" is an age-old marketing tool. Rather, it was the incongruity of the paired items. "Buy a large suitcase and receive a small handbag" made sense. "Buy a large suitcase and get eleven pounds of rice" did not make sense.

Another time, I received several small jars of peanut butter because they came attached to a package of teabags. In certain shops, I noticed that a Hello Kitty tote bag was free with the purchase of a professional-quality camera. I once acquired several pairs of men's large athletic socks, which came free when I bought a pair of women's shoes. When I asked about swapping the socks for a women's pair—or at least smaller sized men's socks—the employees gave me a bewildered look and informed me these were the only free socks they had.

The most absurd "freebie-combo" I saw was a deal at a drugstore in which customers who purchased a certain amount of toothpaste could then buy discounted Coca-Cola. Shouldn't it be the other way around? Buy the Coca-Cola and receive discounted toothpaste because of the overload of sugar on the tooth enamel?

And this soda-and-toothpaste display sat on the checkout counter next to a package of lamb placenta. I found it an unpleasant experience all around.

***

One day I was standing in a supermarket checkout lane behind people who were willing to put in the extra time and effort to maximize the freebies. The group of three in front of me looked like a well-to-do young couple and a mother/mother-in-law. This store had a promotion whereby if you made a purchase over a certain amount, you would receive a free tote bag.

Though these three people were together, they began to meticulously arrange their merchandise in an attempt to divide it into three separate purchases. Since they had so few items, this became a matter of attaining an exact sum for each grouping. The cashier scanned one item, pushing the total too far over the necessary minimum purchase to receive the free bag. The trio removed that item and tried a lesser-priced item.

Like a game-show challenge, this happened over and over until they finally arrived at the right combination of separate purchases to receive three free bags. It also seemed important to them to pay with exact change, even though I spied larger bills in their wallets. Each time a final total rang up, they sorted through their various pockets and purses, carefully counting coins and pooling their resources. A flurry of conversation accompanied this arduous process, though I understood none of it.

I caught the eye of the salesclerk more than once, and I offered her an amused smile, hoping to ward off her frustration with these customers. I was in no hurry and was enjoying the drama unfolding before me. Eventually, the party of three happily departed with a few groceries, three free tote bags, and fewer coins in their wallets.

While placing my items on the checkout counter, I smiled again at the clerk and waved my hand in dismissal when she apologized for the lengthy wait. She then proceeded to offer *me* a free tote bag.

Perhaps I should have inquired about free rice—except that I already had five kilos on hand.

***

I love rice and most other Hong Kong cuisine, but I'll always miss the food of my homeland, particularly around the holidays. The Thanksgiving celebration with American friends I enjoyed my first year in Hong Kong became a long-standing tradition I eagerly anticipated each fall. But I also adopted a second tradition—eating an international dinner on Thanksgiving weekend with a large group of people from a variety of countries. This eclectic feast usually included spring rolls, noodles and sticky rice, pizza and spaghetti, chicken enchiladas and green salad, along with turkey, mashed potatoes, and pumpkin pie.

On one such occasion, two women from Sri Lanka, who had arrived in Hong Kong just the day before, sat quietly alone in a corner, studying the food on their plates. Sitting down next to them, I began chatting with one of them who spoke English.

"What is a Thanksgiving?" she asked me. "It's an American festival, yes?"

"Yes, it's an American holiday." I responded, then launched into a detailed tribute to Thanksgiving culinary delights. "We always eat turkey. Well, some people bake ham. And usually some potatoes and green beans. Maybe rolls and cranberry sauce. Pie for dessert. Especially pumpkin and pecan pies."

"No," she said when I paused. "What is the history of this holiday? *Why* do you celebrate?"

"Oh. Um..."

Visions of grade-school plays filled my mind. Headbands with protruding construction-paper feathers. A black cardboard hat with a yellow buckle painted on the front. A white-and-black Pilgrim frock. My mind crawled along. What exactly was a Pilgrim? Something about *Niña*, *Pinta*, and *Santa Maria*? No, that was Columbus, who sailed the ocean blue in 1492... oh, the *Mayflower*! That was how the Pilgrims reached America. The Indians taught them how to plant corn. Were we allowed to call them Indians anymore? They weren't from India, of course. Why was I so terrible at recalling basic history?

"Well, um, a long time ago, some people moved to America." For reasons unknown, I slipped into my Special English Voice, though this woman spoke impeccable British English. "They were very hungry and were dying."

"They came from England, yes?" she remarked politely.

"Oh, um, yeah, they were from England. Then they came to America. But they didn't know how to grow food or survive. Then the... uh... Native... Indian people came along and taught them how to plant food. And they lived. And they were happy. So, they had a big meal to give thanks."

A Chinese friend sitting nearby eloquently stepped in to my rescue. "The feast was held at the conclusion of harvest season, so there was plenty to eat and be thankful for. Americans recall this story and celebrate each November."

"Yes, harvest," I nodded. "We celebrate harvest."

The Sri Lankan woman asked about the date. "Is it always the twenty-fifth of November?"

At least I knew this one. "No, it's always on a Thursday in late November. It's always the third Thursday—no, the fourth Thursday—wait, is this the fourth week of the month already? Anyway, it's always on a Thursday in November." I trailed off. "Mostly we just eat. And eat. And eat." I patted my stomach and noticed an awkward pause.

"Here, let me clear your plate for you," I offered quickly. She smiled sweetly as my Chinese friend began chatting intelligently on another topic.

It's the little things. The details of history and culture that are so important, yet so rarely referenced in my own culture that I often forget. Lessons learned in primary school that sadly fade from my adult mind.

I can recount in glorious detail every dish my mother cooked for Thanksgiving. But what is the origin of the holiday? Why do we celebrate? These are the kinds of stories that stitch our cultures together and make us who we are. And the stories behind the celebrations are the elements I most love to learn about other nationalities.

Clearly, though, I need to brush up on my homeland's history so I can explain it like a true American. But I maintain that pie will always be an integral part of my culture and its celebrations.

CHAPTER 30

MONKEYS AND STEPLADDERS

A friend was visiting me from the United States. Together we decided to explore the Ten Thousand Buddhas Monastery and Temple, which is located in Sha Tin, a district in the New Territories. We set out energetically one morning as the sun peeked through the clouds. The air felt heavy with heat and humidity as we took a short walk from the train station to where we could see the temple clinging to the side of a forested mountain.

The formidable journey uphill had been made easier by the installation of several outdoor escalators. One of these brought us to an area consisting of three-walled "rooms"—niches about twenty feet wide and ten feet deep. Inside these rooms were hundreds of plaques hanging floor-to-ceiling on the walls, each representing a deceased person. Every plaque contained a short obituary and a location number. In the center of each room sat a metal table on which to burn incense or place offerings of fruit.

We continued our upward hike past makeshift stands selling fruit, incense sticks, and paper effigies for use in ancestor worship. This was a weekday morning, so the temple area remained deserted.

My friend and I snapped photos of the leafy countryside as we came to an area with more of these rooms.

Several people were placing fruit offerings on tables. Suddenly, there was a minor commotion in one section. A man and a woman were waving their arms in apparent irritation. Not understanding their Cantonese, I thought they were upset with each other—an uncommon sight in the serene, peaceful atmosphere of a Buddhist temple.

Then a flash of movement caught my eye. A monkey. Then two monkeys. The fruit offerings were too enticing for the wild macaques to ignore. In the blink of an eye, these mischievous creatures had snatched a red apple and a bright-yellow bunch of bananas. My friend and I laughed in delight even as I wondered how those who brought the offerings felt about the creatures. Sneaking around the corner of the temple, we continued photographing the monkeys' antics. By now, the man and woman had lost interest and resumed their duties.

I suspect this sort of situation happens often, likely multiple times a day, as the surrounding forests are filled with such greedy rapscallions. But what may have been a nuisance to the monastery employees and worshipers brought delightful amusement to us.

"Just another day in Hong Kong," I told my friend with a smile and shrug.

***

Even after I'd lived in Hong Kong for several years, day-to-day situations could still be trying—or sometimes entertaining. For instance, after suffering from slow internet for a while, I decided to upgrade my system. The internet technician was scheduled to come between 10:00 a.m. and 1:00 p.m., so I took a few hours off work to be home during that time.

Around 11:00 a.m., I received a phone call from the internet company employee. Though I couldn't understand all of his Cantonese, I realized he was telling me he'd arrive around 1:30 or 2:00 p.m.

"Okay?" he concluded.

No, this was not okay.

"Two-o'clock, okay," he added.

"No! My appointment was between ten and one," I argued back. "After one is not okay."

"One-thirty or two," he stated with finality.

"No, no! Not okay," I exclaimed in Cantonese, my voice rising.

"Okay. See you at two." With that, he hung up.

Frustrated, I called the company's hotline. I finally reached a person who understood my problem.

"I will call the technician and ask if he can come earlier," she said. "He'll call you first."

"No. He can't speak English, and I'm very sorry that I cannot understand Cantonese," I responded with frustration. "Please send someone who speaks a bit of English and have him come during my scheduled appointment time, which is between eleven and one."

Irritated at my own boorish behavior, yet exasperated at the load of work awaiting me at my office, I hung up with a groan. A half hour later, another man who spoke a little English called to inform me he'd come right away.

And he did.

Without even setting foot in my flat, he began inspecting the cables in the hallway of my building. Because the wires were installed above the doors, he asked for a stepladder. I offered him one of my dining table chairs, which had already undergone repair and was not altogether stable.

"Be careful," I admonished in Cantonese.

The chair proved too short. The technician indicated the need for a ladder. I said I didn't have a ladder. A tall stool? No, I didn't have a stool. Anything else? No, I had nothing else.

With a sigh, he slipped into the stairwell. When he returned, he was dragging the large plastic rubbish bin. The height was suitable, but the brittle lid threatened to collapse. I instinctively moved closer to help in case he fell, then realized the needlessness of my action. This guy likely climbed atop rickety chairs, uneven stepladders, and flimsy rubbish bins every day. He didn't fear a broken lid or the possibility of tumbling into a trashcan. After all, this was Hong Kong, where people are astonishingly resourceful, making do with whatever is on hand. Apparently, it's not an overly litigious society either.

After a twenty-second inspection from atop the garbage bin, the technician descended, returned the bin to the stairwell, and rattled off his assessment, which I didn't understand. With another sigh, he pulled out his mobile phone and began typing a message in Chinese. He ran it through a translation app, then handed me his phone. I read an unintelligible group of English words constructed into "sentences" in which verbs and nouns jumbled together indiscriminately. Several phrases contained technical terminology I'd never heard.

After reading it twice, I shrugged and gave him a confused look. He pointed to my phone sitting on the table nearby and informed me that I should "call Chinese friend." I obeyed. After a few conversations, in which he and I passed my phone back and forth while speaking to my local friend, I arrived at the understanding that nothing could be done. My front door frame required a hole drilled through it, and then I'd need to book a technician to return to install wiring.

No high-speed internet for me that day. And I would have to make another appointment. At which time I'd have to do this all over again. Without a stepladder or translator.

I really need to learn Cantonese. Or at least purchase a ladder.

CHAPTER 31

CORNUCOPIA AND FOLKLORE

I find it difficult to accept advice I don't understand. This includes old wives' tales—those bits of wisdom passed down over time wherein the original purpose is forgotten or no longer exists. Must we really wait a certain amount of time after eating before we jump in the lake to swim? If I pluck out a gray hair, will two actually grow back in its place? Such folklore within my own culture is not easy to swallow—and even more so when it comes from a different culture.

Hong Kong is a cornucopia of various people groups mixed together, so I'm not always sure of the origin of the counsel I'm receiving. Asians seem to agree on one nugget of wisdom, though. Putting ice in your drink is unhealthy. If you drink a cup of cold water immediately after a meal, the food oils may solidify in your body, slowing down digestion and maybe even causing a heart attack or cancer. Adding ice to beverages increases the risk, so we should drink only hot or warm water. I admit I routinely ignore this admonition.

As a youngish person residing in a culture steeped in folk remedies and surrounded by more knowledgeable locals, it's a guarantee I'll get fussed at or reprimanded for something at some point. Of course every people group has such bits of sagacity that trickle down from generation to generation, which may or may not be based on scientifically-proven principles. We often accept such theories simply because it's what we've been told since childhood.

On the other hand, in today's Google-driven world we sometimes view cultural wisdom with skepticism, turning instead to websites that specialize in myth-breaking experiments and explanations. Whether science should always be elevated over conventional knowledge is another matter. It reminds me that "everything you're sure is right can be wrong in another place."[15]

I confess I initially viewed Chinese medicine on the whole as dubious as it did not fit with my preconceived understanding of medical practices. But during the years I've lived in Asia, I've heard numerous first-hand testimonies of its benefits. If people have utilized this methodology for thousands of years and continue to do so, it must be effective at least to some degree. Interestingly, when I moved to Hong Kong, I purchased health insurance through a well-known international company. The options I was offered included the choice of coverage for Western medicine, Chinese medicine, or both.

I've learned that traditional Chinese medicine practitioners believe our bodies must be balanced in all ways, particularly regarding the substances we eat. Experts characterize all food as either hot or cold, not in reference to its temperature but in how it affects the body. I previously thought of orange juice as being refreshing and effective in fighting flu or a head cold. But when I visited a Hong Kong doctor for this ailment, he instructed me to

[15] Kingsolver, Barbara, *The Poisonwood Bible* (New York: Harper Perennial, 2005), 606.

avoid orange juice because it was "hot." This is the yin and yang, the life forces, the energies in the body that must be proportionate.

There is a wealth of advice for pregnant women, some of which is unusual in my Western mind. For instance, women abstain from eating snake while they are expecting as this could cause the newborn to have a scaly appearance. They should refrain from yelling to prevent the child from having a bad disposition. Expectant mothers should also avoid overly happy occasions, such as weddings and birthdays, or excessively sad ones, such as funerals. These extreme emotions could upset the body's qi (life force) or adversely impact the heart and liver. I even once heard that pregnant women should avoid looking at a monkey, but I have no idea why.

I am even more perplexed by the various beliefs about a mother's activities post-birth, which many Hong Kong women have shared with me. Some believe that for thirty to forty days after the birth, the mother should not take a shower or brush her teeth. She should not go outside lest she catch a cold. (Or perhaps this is to save the general public from being exposed to the stench of unwashed skin and un-brushed teeth.) She shouldn't switch on the air conditioner or open the windows but must keep warm by staying in bed under layers of blankets regardless of the season. And, again, she must avoid icy drinks and cold food.

I suspect most of these traditions have an ounce of truth and a pound of folklore. It is logical that a woman who recently gave birth should stay home, rest, and avoid undue exertion. Keeping the new mother and baby away from crowded public areas decreases exposure to sickness and germs. But not brushing the teeth? I can't figure that one out.

My personal experience with post-birth traditions occurred when I was a guest in the home of a family who had recently welcomed the arrival of a new grandchild. Many Hong Kong mothers-in-law cook a special soup-like dish for the new mother called "trotters and ginger in sweetened vinegar." According to Chinese thought, the ingredients—which are, as the name suggests, pork knuckles, ginger, vinegar, and hard-boiled eggs—will help the woman's body regain strength and vitality. Traditionally, a huge pot of this concoction would be prepared, then left to sit on the stovetop for hours or days, allowing the meat and sliced ginger to soak up the full flavor of the vinegar.

My friend invited me and others to her home where she served us this Cantonese-style dish as a way of celebrating the birth of her grandchild. Unlike a comparable American celebration, neither the baby nor the new parents were present. I found the age-old custom fascinating but was less enthusiastic about the taste. The pork was tender and delicious, but the ginger and vinegar flavors were overwhelmingly strong. And I decided it would be more enjoyable to celebrate a baby's birth by actually seeing the baby.

* * *

Various traditions, folklore, myths, and rituals abound in Hong Kong even as the city is known for cutting-edge technology and fashion. The contemporary culture stands easily alongside centuries of time-honored customs. At the base of a shiny, glass-plated skyscraper, an elderly street sweeper uses a homemade bamboo broom and a dustbin fashioned from a recycled tin can. Developers create an office building fitted with the latest technological advances, yet also follow the advice of a Feng Shui master before the floor plan is finalized. A multi-story architectural gem contains a giant "window" in the center to allow the spirit of the dragon—who ostensibly lives on the mountain behind the building—to come and go at will.

A woman chats on her new mobile phone while hanging laundry out to dry on a public pedestrian bridge. Fishermen aboard an ancient sampan paddle through the Hong Kong harbor, rocked by the wake of a massive five-star cruise ship. Within a few blocks, one can purchase the latest Fendi purse for thousands of dollars or peruse a local market that offers live seafood or fresh fruit and vegetables for mere pocket change.

This is a city filled with inconsistency.

Meanwhile, as I'm still learning to navigate the deep waters of an ancient culture, I'll simply smile and continue on my merry ice-cold-water-drinking way—always hoping I can avoid committing too many societal blunders.

CHAPTER 32

HOSPITALS AND PUNCHLINES

"What if the machine only speaks Chinese?" I silently panicked as I prepared for a CT scan in a local hospital. The nurse had already exited the room after instructing me to "do what the machine says." Mercifully, this scanner was bilingual. The recorded voice spoke both Cantonese and delightful Aussie English.

In the United States, one must be deathly ill before gaining admittance to a hospital. In Hong Kong, the hospital keeps patients far longer than necessary and for the most insignificant reasons. An ingrown toenail requires an overnight stay. Literally. This is not a figure of speech. They hospitalized me overnight—the night *before* the surgery—to have a toenail addressed. Staying in a ward filled with sick or injured patients when I had no discernible illness was an odd experience. It felt more like a regrettable hotel stay.

I've never experienced hospitalization in America, but I've been sent to the hospital several times since moving to Hong Kong. These are some of my observations about the local medical system.

First, communication is difficult. Apart from my inability to speak or understand much Cantonese, the medical personnel wear surgical masks at all times, hiding three-quarters of their faces. In fact, since Hong Kong experienced SARS (Severe Acute Respiratory Syndrome) in 2003, surgical masks have been worn by everyone in hospitals—doctors, nurses, orderlies, and guests. Wearing a mask when one feels sick or one is fearful of catching an illness is an ordinary part of daily life in the city. (Note: with the arrival of COVID-19, masks became mandatory for all city residents at all times.)

Medical personnel also pronounce terminology in the British way or use British vocabulary with which I am unfamiliar. Add some Chinglish, a bit of medical jargon, and consider that the patient has taken some sort of medication, and it becomes a terribly bewildering situation. I'm grateful that I haven't been hospitalized for anything serious. After all, who knows what questions I could have misunderstood or answered incorrectly?

Nurse: "Are you the patient who's here to have an elbow removed?"

Me: "Ummm… yes?"

Secondly, a visit to some medical clinics make me feel I've stepped back in time. Most Hong Kong physicians have their own office, where they wait for a nurse to escort the patient to a chair next to the doctor's desk. Some clinics are newly designed with cheery decor and spotless furniture. Many others appear drab and dark with brown vinyl benches, bare walls, a metal desk, and patient charts with handwritten notes. Medical paraphernalia—a jar of tongue depressors, a blood pressure cuff, a thermometer, a few slides showing physical ailments—mix with office items on the desk, such as a cup of pens, a ruler, stacks of papers, a book or two.

Hospitals—especially public hospitals—also feel like a blast from the past. Narrow hallways, dim lighting, and aqua green or pink walls. Nurses wear traditional uniforms: neatly pressed collared tops, short skirts, thick stockings, white nursing shoes, and—the crowning touch—a cardboard-stiff white nurse's cap. Even the orderlies and janitors wear old-style polyester uniforms. Scrubs are rarely seen.

Thirdly, there is no privacy. When patients are transferred to and from the operating room (called an "operating theater" in this British culture), orderlies transport them in the main public elevator. On more than one occasion while visiting someone in the hospital, I have stepped into a lift and found myself awkwardly pressed up against a gurney carrying a patient still groggy from anesthesia. Visitors, family members, doctors, nurses, hospital staff, and patients frequently share the same lifts.

While privacy regarding personal data is valued and protected in Hong Kong, an astounding number of breaches occur. Once when I was in the patient discharge process while leaving the hospital, I was handed a book in which to sign out. It was a black and red paper notebook that looked like something a fourth-grade teacher would have used fifty years ago to record grades. Other patients' names appeared before mine, and anyone who signed after me could see my full name as well. Coming from a country in which strict privacy laws are mandated throughout the healthcare systems, this took me by surprise.

My hospital experiences have mostly been at private facilities, i.e., covered by personal health insurance. But I occasionally visit patients and friends in public hospitals, which are government-subsidized and affordable. The contrast is vast. In the private hospital, a room has two beds separated by a curtain while a ward has six to eight beds, each separated by a curtain. In a public hospital, as many as thirty beds are crammed into a ward with no curtains available and barely enough space for a guest to stand between the beds.

I was once visiting a lady in a public hospital, and when I leaned over to speak with her, my backside bumped the bed next to hers. Worse, population growth and lagging infrastructure in Hong Kong have created overcrowding in public hospitals, necessitating situations where some patients are relegated to a bed in the hallway.

Fourthly, the hospital feels like a prison from which one cannot escape. In every hospitalization I've experienced in Hong Kong, I've literally begged for release. I always received responses from doctors and nurses such as:

"Just wait. People here can take care of you, so relax. You might as well stay a few more hours."

"The doctor can't come back until her evening shift, so you should remain another night."

"No need to be in such a hurry to leave. One more IV. We want to make sure the medicine is working."

Contrast this with American hospitals, where they may toss you out on the street two hours after having a leg amputated.

***

Even after living in Hong Kong for a number of years, I am still surprised—and very grateful—for the helpfulness of others when they see I'm a lost, confused foreigner. In addition to hospital employees demonstrating kindness, I've also experienced assistance from complete strangers in other contexts.

One afternoon, I attempted to get a few photos printed from my USB drive at a local photo shop. The low-ceilinged store was minuscule, so customers and employees had to sidle around one another to move from the cash register to the printing kiosks along the wall. Making things more crowded, a gargantuan pillar filled the center of the store—apparently holding up the entire shopping mall floor. This was not prime retail space, though it still likely cost tens of thousands of dollars in monthly rent.

After waiting in line, I stepped up to the counter and made my request. I was directed to the first kiosk into which I inserted my memory stick. The computer did not recognize my USB device, so an employee came to help, removing the memory stick and trying it at the next kiosk. When he was drawn away to assist other customers, I began to maneuver the computer menu myself. Despite choosing English, I encountered what appeared to be an error message written in Chinese. I waited. I pushed buttons on the screen. I waited some more. Nothing happened.

Not able to get the attention of any employees, I asked another customer who looked like a university student, "Can you please tell me what this says?"

Instead of answering, she took charge of the machine and endeavored to solve my problem for me. To no avail. I thanked her, then waited until an employee noticed my frustration and came over to assist me.

This employee, a woman, tried my device in machine after machine. Finally, the fifth—and last—kiosk accepted it. The card reader machines looked like relics from the 1990s, and the woman had an array of tricks to get one working. Shove the memory stick in and out of the USB port multiple times, push it to one side, tap on the top, grind her teeth, and stick her tongue out of the corner of her mouth. The problem was clearly not my particular device but the computers themselves.

Eventually, I was able to choose the photos I wanted to print. Retrieving my memory stick, I took the numbered ticket spit out by the machine and proceeded to the checkout counter. After queuing for a few minutes, I approached the same saleswoman who'd helped me before and handed her my ticket. I watched her fill out a duplicate form by hand (apparently, it was now the 1980s) and realized the price was triple what I had expected. I objected. She didn't understand my English, and I was confused by the number of photos for which I was being charged.

We circled through this muddled conversation a few times. I tried to explain that since I'd only chosen a few photos to print, it shouldn't cost that much. Another sympathetic customer entered the conversation, and we collectively ascertained I'd accidentally chosen quadruple prints of each photo. Frustrated with the saleswoman's lack of concern and the machine's performance, I threw up my hands in surrender and agreed to pay the total, which amounted to about US$6 extra. The photos were of my darling oldest nephew, so I could give the duplicate prints to family.

At this point, a third customer stepped forward to assist me. Wearing the uniform of a respectable department store in the same mall, he was efficient, spoke excellent English, and quickly grasped the situation. At first, I declined his help. Those computers were dysfunctional, and I didn't want to spend another fifteen minutes trying to get one of them to accept my disk. But he said I shouldn't be responsible for paying for something I didn't want and insisted that the photo technicians help me remedy the matter. (I'm not sure *they* agreed on this point.)

The entire scene caught the attention of the first employee. Soon two technicians and two customers were helping me. The male employee took over, walking me back to the one functioning kiosk—at which yet another customer was having problems. He asked her to wait, plugged in my USB drive, voided my previous transaction, and guided me successfully through the entire process again.

At last, I paid the money I owed. Before leaving, I walked around and thanked the various customers who'd assisted me. I felt like we'd bonded together during this ordeal and I was now on my farewell tour through the little photo shop.

Sometimes I feel like I live in the punch line of a joke. How many Hong Kongers does it take to assist an ignorant gweilo with a routine task?

CHAPTER 33

THE TORCH AND POTATOES

On a June afternoon, one of my friends and I set out for an adventure. The 2008 Olympics were approaching, and there was a spirit of excitement in the air as the Olympic torch was going to pass through Hong Kong on its way to Beijing.

According to the relevant website, the Olympic flame would make several short trips through strategic—though disconnected—areas of Hong Kong. I wasn't sure how the locations were chosen nor why they weren't linked to each other. It would have made more sense to have one course through which the Olympic torch traversed over a longer period of time.

As it was, there were eight different routes that constituted the torch's relay through Hong Kong with stops and breaks between each leg. Did the marathon runners really need a two-hour lunch break after jogging casually on paved streets, carrying a lightweight stick of fire, pausing for photo-ops, and receiving refreshments from the accompanying motorcade?

My friend and I chose the time and location most convenient to us and headed out into the chaos. Not knowing precisely where we should go, my friend convinced me to follow red-shirted people, since Hong Kong organizers had instructed citizens to wear red as a sign of support and celebration of the Beijing Olympics. I was concerned that many people carrying red paper flags were headed in the opposite direction as us, but this didn't faze my friend.

We rode the train and exited in Tsim Sha Tsui, a district in Kowloon along the harbor. We advanced toward our destination, weaving through a crowd of celebrants to what looked like the entrance to the Avenue of Stars, a pseudo-Hollywood Walk of Fame. It did indeed turn out to be the entrance, but several barricades, a number of police officers, and a crowd of eager onlookers blocked it. Once we wended our way to the front of the crowd, it became clear that no one was being allowed into the promenade area, though this was the intended path of the Olympic torch.

As we were still trying to decipher the situation, a reporter holding a television microphone tapped me on the shoulder and asked if she could interview me. Tugging on my friend's sleeve, I told the reporter, "My friend will do it."

My friend turned around, facing the eager reporter and her camera-toting sidekick. The reporter asked her, "So what do you think of the Olympic torch ceremony?"

"We just arrived and have yet to see anything," my friend replied.

The reporter went on to ask where my friend was from. She responded that she was from the United States but currently lived in Hong Kong. Again, the reporter pressed her for an opinion. My friend repeated that we'd seen nothing yet, then asked, "Do you know where I can go to see the torch? Also, where can I get one of those little red flags?"

The reporter had a look on her face that said, "I'm supposed to be the one asking the questions here!"

As I dissolved into a fit of laughter, our interview promptly ended. Extracting ourselves from the crowd, my friend and I walked over to a policeman and asked him where we should go to see the torch. He first brushed us aside, then pointed vaguely in one direction. When we asked again, he replied that only "guests" were allowed beyond the barricades to view the actual torch procession.

Undaunted, my friend moved on to one of his colleagues, another policeman, and asked the same questions. "Where can I go to see the torch? I came all the way here just to see the torch. Can I be a guest? Can you let me in?"

Unfazed, the second policeman—now joined by several other officers—insisted that no one could pass the barricades. Guests only. I trailed behind as my friend marched off in search of another loophole in the system. As we moved away from the police officers, a young woman holding a thin notebook and pen followed us, trying to get our attention and claiming to be a local journalist. I knew she'd overheard the conversation between us and the officers, and I hoped she might somehow have inside information, so we stopped and turned to face her.

She immediately inquired, "So how do you feel about not getting in to see the torch?"

The absurdity of these common journalistic questions hit me. We evaded the reporter's queries by asking her, "Can you get us in to see the torch?"

When her answer was no, we moved on. Further down the promenade, we encountered another barricade, this one less crowded and guarded by a gentleman in a business suit wearing an

Olympic placard around his neck. Thinking this was someone with clout, my friend strode up to him and implored, "Can I go in to see the torch?"

When given a negative answer, my friend proceeded down the now-well-worn path of pleas. "We came to see the torch. We were told we could see the torch if we came here. We want to cheer and greet the Olympic torch. Where can we see it? How can we get in?"

The man refused to allow us to enter, though a smile played around the corners of his eyes and mouth. Clearly, he found amusement in my friend's passionate attempt to worm her way into the viewing area. But he repeated firmly, "Guests only."

My friend switched tactics. "I want to be a guest. How can I be a guest?"

Despite my friend's high-pitched voice and puppy-dog-pleading eyes, the man refused us entry. "Only people who received an invitation can come through. I cannot allow anyone else to come behind the barricade."

"Why is this so?" inquired my friend.

"These are my orders," the man replied.

"But why?" asked my friend sadly.

"This is my job. I don't know why. I have to follow my orders," he said again. With a smile, he waved us on.

Spotting a crowd forming at the end of a sidewalk nestled between two buildings, we zigzagged our way through the throngs of people until we found ourselves up against yet another barricade guarded by three other police officers. My friend embarked once more on her verbal entreaty to be allowed in, this time taking advantage of the fact that these officers looked very young and persuadable.

"Please, can't I be a guest? The website said the public could see the torch, but now I'm told only guests. Only guests. Why? I want to cheer and wave a flag for the Olympic torch!"

The young officers grinned shyly, eyed the crowd behind us, then turned to each other, talking in Cantonese. But they shook their heads no. Their job was to keep people from passing the barricade. "Guests only. Very sorry, but guests only."

Realizing they felt badly for having to turn us away, my friend told them, "I know this is not your fault. You are small potatoes. I am small potatoes too, or else I would be in there watching the torch."

The young officers chuckled, and the crowd pressing in behind us burst into laughter. Small potatoes, indeed. We all were.

Admitting defeat, my friend kindly said to the officers, "I am not upset with you. I know you are doing your job. But I am sad that I cannot see the torch."

One officer nodded his head in agreement, saying, "I am sad too. I would also like to see the torch."

"Thank you. You understand. But I took off work today so I could come see the torch," my friend pointed out. "At least you're getting paid to stand here and not see the torch."

The young officer grinned at her logic.

And so we waited. Realizing there was a meager chance we might get a peek at the flame as it passed through the gap in front of us, we valiantly held our spot, crammed up against the barricade that had to be moved back and forth as workmen carried equipment in and out. Other eager onlookers pushed their way to the front where we were, attempting to usurp the minuscule amount of viewing space we had. Periodically, a gasp from the crowd behind us erupted as a media crew raised a microphone boom over the Avenue of Stars in the distance.

Finally, standing on tiptoes with craned necks and the crowd surging behind us, we caught a glimpse of a dark-windowed van, out of which several cameras were aimed, crawling up the Avenue of Stars and surrounded by a fleet of motorcycle police officers. In a span of two seconds, the runner carrying the symbol of international unity found only in the Olympic Games passed through our field of vision. An orange flame was barely visible from our distant vantage point. It flitted by so quickly I was hardly able to snap a photo.

But we saw it.

We saw the torch.

We small potatoes had welcomed the 2008 Beijing Summer Olympic Games.

CHAPTER 34

CRACKERS AND CULTURES

My favorite Christmas traditions in Hong Kong began several years after moving there. On Christmas Day, I was invited to the home of a Hong Kong family who have a British background, so their customs were slightly different than my own upbringing. Among them was the Christmas cracker, a delightful way of kicking off the festivities.

For my fellow Americans, a British Christmas cracker is actually a decorated cardboard tube slightly shorter than a paper towel roll and shaped to resemble a large piece of wrapped candy. We gathered around the table, crossed our arms at the elbows, and grasped the end of a different cracker in each hand. On the count of three, everyone pulled their end of the cracker, resulting in a loud pop—the "crack"—similar to the noise of a cap gun. Each cracker broke unevenly, leaving one person with the larger portion while the other got only the broken remnant. It reminded me of the turkey wishbone tradition in America where one person gets the short end and the other "wins."

Each cracker contained a small toy, a tissue-paper hat, and a slip of paper on which was written a joke. The person who "won" the larger section of two crackers shared the contents with someone else who got nothing. Everyone, adults included, put on the papery crowns. Then we took turns reading the jokes, which were holiday-themed riddles (Q: Where does Santa keep his money? A: In a snowbank). For a few moments, all of us were children again, modeling our tissue tiaras, trading trinkets, and groaning at silly puns.

Christmas dinner was then served, complete with turkey, ham, dressing, corn on the cob, roasted potatoes, and cranberry sauce. The elements of the meal were comparable to an American Thanksgiving or Christmas feast, but the methods of cooking and specific ingredients were dissimilar. British Christmas potatoes were not mashed. The dressing contained chestnuts and was rather sweet. It was also formed into uniform slices like meatloaf rather than in loose spoonfuls. The cranberry sauce was chunky, containing actual cranberries, compared to the classic American version, which comes jellied and molded into the unsophisticated shape of a tin can. There were also Brussels sprouts, a vegetable I'd never tasted before moving to Hong Kong but have grown to love.

This particular gathering of friends consisted of people from both sides of the Atlantic, so we also indulged in American desserts—fudge, frosted sugar cookies, chocolate-dipped pretzels, gingerbread men, and more. Soon the inevitable food-induced coma set in. We lounged on the sofas, exchanged gifts, then sat back and watched the kids play with their new gadgets while we sipped hot drinks.

Later that evening, I journeyed home, took a nap, then spent most of the night hours on a video chat with my family in the United States, who were enjoying their Christmas morning in Central Standard Time. My stocking had already arrived in a package from

Texas, thanks to my generous and thoughtful parents. I dove into it, starting the holiday all over again.

Of course I pretended it was a new day so I could eat yet another batch of chocolate goodies, guilt-free.

***

Ultimately, a greater knowledge of Asia has caused me to understand Americans—and myself—on a deeper level. If adapting to a new culture requires making connections between the known and unknown, the known also comes under scrutiny. Aspects of my own upbringing and background of which I was previously unaware have now become fodder for examination.

For instance, Americans veer toward individuality while Asians tend toward conformity. In my American mind, the attribute of independence is valued, and my overseas relocation reflects this. To an Asian mind, my behavior is confusing. Hong Kongers will ask me, "You moved here alone? Where is your family? Why would you leave your home to come here?"

In other situations, I feel frustrated when an individual refuses to speak up or act assertively. Yet that person is simply complying with their cultural norms. To put it idiomatically, an American would state: "The squeaky wheel gets the grease." To which the Asian would counter: "The nail that sticks out gets hammered down."[16]

Both ends of the spectrum hold value and cultural richness. A society that promotes social harmony and upholds familial relationships often functions in a more peaceful manner than that in

[16] Weiner, Eric, *The Geography of Bliss: One Grump's Search for the Happiest Places in the World* (New York: Twelve, 2008), 179-80.

which individuality and personal desires are emphasized. Still, in a society that values cohesion above all else, many people ignore personal complaints and frustrations until they reach a boiling point and an emotional blowup destroys that superficial peace.

Conversely, a grievous trait of many citizens in my motherland is a sense of entitlement—an ugly, bulging-eyed monster that asserts its will in much of my own attitudes and thinking. The air-conditioning doesn't work properly, and I insist it be fixed immediately. The bus driver has the radio blaring. I dislike the music and have a headache, so I wish I could ask him to turn down the volume. In the building across the street, a dog barks continuously after 10:00 p.m., and I expect its owners to take action to stop this.

But when I mention my complaints to local friends, I often receive disinterested shrugs. "This is Hong Kong. This is how things are here. There's nothing you can do about it."

In these and other situations, I need to pause and examine myself. Why do I feel this way? What cultural biases are affecting my view of this matter? Is this a situation in which I must offer my opinion, or is it wiser to submit to the pervading norm of this environment and address the issue from another angle?

There is a certain sense of peace attained when I employ the "shrug and be indifferent" approach in an annoying situation. This requires surrendering my framework of perfection and reinterpreting what is an actual need versus what is merely a perceived personal right. Perhaps I've begun the shift from being an ungreased squeaky wheel to a nail already hammered down.

Nevertheless, I feel I am entitled to ice in my drinks. This should be a fundamental human right along with life, liberty, and the pursuit of happiness.

CHAPTER 35

HOME

As a summer vacation in the United States drew to a close, I bade farewell to my family and successfully traversed the horrors of airport security checkpoints. Since I'd surrendered my beverage at the x-ray machines, I began looking around for a place to purchase water. Locating a newsstand near my gate, I grabbed a bottle of water and a bit of candy—Reese's Pieces, a guilty pleasure often unavailable in Hong Kong.

The cashier scanned my items. The total came to $3.40. Wanting to offload some of my American coins, I pulled out eight quarters and handed them to the woman. She looked at me and said, "The total is three-forty."

I nodded, impatiently reshuffling the bag on my shoulder. Then I realized she was still looking at me. She repeated, "It's three dollars and forty cents."

Glancing at the pile of coins in her hand, I thought, "Why are some Texans so dense? I've given her four dollars."

Pause. Prior to this moment, I'd spent several weeks in the United States, during which time I'd made numerous successful transactions with American currency. But now it wasn't yet 7:00 a.m., and I was desperately low on sleep. I always struggle with math. An American quarter is similar in size to a Hong Kong fifty-cent coin. Those were my only excuses. And how pitiful they were.

Our cash register standoff continued. I squinted at the clerk. She stared at me. By now a line of customers had begun to grow behind me. With an air of annoyance, the woman placed the quarters on the counter in groups of four.

"The total is three dollars and forty cents," she repeated with slow deliberation. "This is two dollars."

Finally, it all clicked in my brain, and I realized my embarrassing mistake. Painfully aware of all the people standing behind me observing the situation, I grabbed a twenty-dollar bill from my wallet, thrust it into her hands, and hastily gathered up the quarters. I probably had $3.40 in coinage, but I didn't dare try to calculate it then.

The cashier handed me the change. Collecting my purchases, I edged away from the counter and blurted out to everyone within earshot, "I'm sorry! I'm not from here!"

I'm not from here? This was the nation of my birth. Indeed, the very state in which I'd lived the first two-and-a-half decades of my life. I'd just made an odd and confusing situation even more awkward by claiming—in a decidedly Texas accent—that I'm not American.

"I haven't resided in the States in several years. My skills in quickly calculating the local monetary system are severely out of practice. It's dawn, and I'm so darn tired!" These would have been more accurate statements.

As I settled into a chair near my gate, sipping my hard-earned bottle of water, I consoled myself. I love living in Hong Kong. One look at my Western nose and green eyes and people around me instinctively make allowances for my blunders and gaffes. It's okay for me to be stupid there.

***

T.S. Eliot once said, "The end of all exploring will be to arrive where we started and know the place for the first time."[17]

Returning to the United States, even for a few weeks of vacation, presents a whole new set of challenges. It requires a mental channel change as I shed my Hong Kong/Chinese/British phrases and mannerisms and go back to being an American among other Americans.

Expats live in an alternate reality, a sort of parallel universe somewhere between their present home and their country of origin. Perhaps I'm a different person depending on my geographical location. For instance, I'm generally a frugal person, which my Hong Kong friends may not know since I tend to shop at the pricier Western grocery stores where I can locate familiar products.

One of my closest American friends in Hong Kong moved back to the United States where I've visited her frequently. We've discovered unexpected differences about each other that we were unaware of in the Eastern Hemisphere. In Hong Kong, she didn't enjoy eating out in restaurants. When we got together in America, I learned she actually likes dining out. It was the noisy, crowded conditions of Hong Kong restaurants that she didn't prefer.

---

[17] Eliot, T. S., "Little Gidding," *The Complete Poems and Plays, 1909-1950* (New York: Harcourt Brace Jovanovich, 1971), 145.

Shortly after I moved to Hong Kong, a new American friend paid me an amusing compliment: "I'd be friends with you even in America."

There is truth to that. There are times when expats choose to build relationships with other expats simply because they have a shared commonality—the expat life. In our native environment, we might not necessarily pick the same companions.

Despite this alternate existence, I revel in the delights of America during my holidays home. Television in English. Dairy Queen Blizzards. Driving on the right-hand side of the road. The ability to easily exchange unwanted items after purchase. Free drink refills. Chick-fil-A. Comical commercials. The scent of fresh-cut grass. Tex-Mex food. Wide aisles at the grocery store. Clear skies without pollution. Unlimited ice for my drinks.

I become an obsessive eavesdropper when I arrive in the United States simply because I can understand the conversations around me. In Texas, I enjoy spontaneous exchanges with strangers while standing in line at the supermarket. "The rain is really comin' down hard out there, in' it?"

I enjoy returning to a corner of the globe where everyday courtesies from strangers are normal. Opening a door for someone else. Letting another step into the elevator first. Saying thank you or hearing "Yessir" or "No, ma'am" all around me. I appreciate salesclerks and store employees in the United States who go out of their way for the customer—as in, they literally move out of the way when a customer walks by.

Or the unique way Southerners have of acknowledging another car when they pass on a two-lane highway or neighborhood street, the index finger just slightly lifting off the top of the steering wheel. The "Texas finger wave," as we call it there. And pickup trucks. There's actually a pickup in my Hong Kong neighborhood, and I find myself staring at it often. It seems so incongruous in the Asian urban jungle.

I am amused when I visit my parents and hear or experience a show-and-tell of all the latest critters who've taken up residence in their backyard. A family of owls. Squirrels. An unwelcome skunk. Several possums. Deer that eat their plants. The neighbor's dog who is named after a Republican politician. (To this day I've no idea if the name is meant as a tribute or a slam.) Altogether, more creatures than I've seen in a year in Hong Kong.

I enjoy the blue skies, trees, wide-open spaces, sunrises and sunsets (well, no, I don't actually wake up for the sunrise), lakes, and the stars at night, which really are big and bright deep in the heart of Texas.

Coming back to America means freedom of speech. By which I mean not having to filter out my Texas accent, Americanisms, Seinfeld references, idioms, and other figures of speech.

Yet returning to the United States also triggers a sort of reverse culture shock common to expats around the globe. Why are Americans so often ethnocentric, arrogant, or wasteful? Why does the evening news focus only on local and national matters, excluding international concerns? Do people in North America even realize there's another entire world out there?

But this is unfair. I'm holding my compatriots to the standards of one who has experienced these things. I'm expecting them to behave as others behave—specifically like those who've had firsthand exposure and insight into other cultures. I don't even realize I've changed until I return to my home country and begin to see that I don't fit in the way I used to. It's not right for me to assume those at home have also transformed.

And what is home? When I'm in Hong Kong, I speak of home in reference to America, to Texas, to my family. While traveling within the United States, I say I'm ready to get back home, meaning my own bed and flat in Hong Kong. Ridiculously, home seems to be wherever I am not.

Returning to America is difficult because it reminds me how markedly I've changed. Coming back to Hong Kong is also challenging because I realize anew how much I miss my family, my friends, my homeland, and my own culture. Sometimes I feel like I live in an ambiguous state, unclear of where I truly belong.

But I wouldn't trade it for anything.

Despite the challenges and obstacles associated with relocating to the opposite hemisphere, the benefits far outweigh the troubles. Cross-cultural living—particularly in a diverse international city like Hong Kong—brings a freshness and richness to life not found elsewhere. With its unique blend of cultures, customs, and languages, Hong Kong offers a wide array of experiences and encounters.

I'm acquainted with a Vietnamese woman who was one of the "boat people" who fled Vietnam after the war in 1975 to seek refuge in Hong Kong. I know a Pakistani Christian who left his family and village because of religious persecution and ended up in our city. A young African man—who lost his family, was forced to engage in civil war as a child soldier, and through a complicated set of tragic circumstances ended up as a teenaged refugee in Hong Kong—has become like a little brother to me. I've met students from Mainland China who ask questions about Christianity, government, and politics. Countless Filipino women have entered my life, teaching me lessons in humility, graciousness, and servanthood. A sweet-natured Nepalese woman befriended me, a woman who emerged from a frightful marriage, barely alive and forever scarred from attempting to take her own life.

I grew close to a family from New Zealand who frequently demonstrated kindness and encouragement to me. Two young Kazakhstani students taught me to appreciate lively folk music from their country. A South African-born man and his Chinese wife have supported me in challenging times. A Ukrainian woman has become a trusted confidante. I've become friends with people from Malaysia, Canada, Indonesia, Singapore, Germany, India, Laos, Mongolia, Panama, Thailand, England, Myanmar, and Australia.

Each of these people, who represent cultures and worlds entirely different from my own, have enriched and broadened my worldview. I will forever see my life and my surroundings through the lenses of this international perspective. I have changed because of the people, cultures, and traditions that have touched and shaped my own existence.

This is cross-cultural living at its best.

This is Hong Kong.

ACKNOWLEDGEMENTS

I owe thanks to many, beginning with my parents, siblings, grandparents, and other extremely biased family members who read early drafts of this book and offered effusive (perhaps obligatory) compliments.

Several friends read versions of my material and gave helpful feedback, and I'm pleased to report our friendships are still intact: Lela Chan, Alice Kingman, Nancy Lucenay, Holly Sprink, Helen Tsang, Andy and Sherlynn Wong, and Barry Yen.

Thanks also to Jeanette Windle, my editor, who helped shape a jumbled manuscript into a well-organized book. That readers stuck around to the end is a tribute to her work.

Thank you to my dear friend, Michelle Miralles, an amazing graphic designer who willingly took on the book design, offered endless advice, and didn't laugh at my sample scribbles. And much appreciation to her talented daughter, Isabelle Li, whose illustrations grace the cover.

I'm so grateful to my best friend in Hong Kong, Leah Presley, who read multiple drafts of this manuscript and supported me in this 16-year writing journey, as well as in the greater journey of life.

Lastly, I'm thankful to my best friend in America, Michelle Essex. Without her, my writing would still be filed away on a hard drive, and readers would never know who led me on the adventure of viewing the Olympic torch.

ABOUT THE AUTHOR

Angela D. French moved to Hong Kong in 2005, where she accepted a position as music director in an international church. She grew up in a small town in central Texas (United States), where she spent most of her childhood reading, writing, making music, and speaking American English.

Angela earned a Bachelor of Music from the University of Mary Hardin-Baylor (Belton, Texas), a Master of Music from Baylor University (Waco, Texas), and a Master of Divinity from George W. Truett Theological Seminary (Baylor University).

So... This is Hong Kong is her first full-length publication.

Printed in Great Britain
by Amazon

16670122R00128